THE SECRET OF BROKENNESS

ORENCIA R. BULZE

THE SECRET OF BROKENNESS

Copyright © 2019 by ORENCIA R. BULZE

"Scripture taken from The Message. Copyright © 1993, 1994, 1995, 1996, 2000, 2001, 2002. Used by permission of NavPress Publishing Group." Holy Bible, New Living Translation, copyright © ©1996, 2004, 2007, 2013, 2015 by Tyndale House Foundation. Used by permission of Tyndale House Publishers Inc., Carol Stream, Illinois 60188. All rights reserved. THE HOLY BIBLE, NEW INTERNATIONAL VERSION®, NIV® Copyright © 1973, 1978, 1984, 2011 by Biblica, Inc.® Used by permission. All rights reserved worldwide. Scripture quotations marked HCSB are taken from the Holman Christian Standard Bible®, Copyright © 1999, 2000, 2002, 2003, 2009 by Holman Bible Publishers. Used by permission. Holman Christian Standard Bible®, Holman CSB®, and HCSB® are federally registered trademarks of Holman Bible Publishers.

ALL RIGHTS RESERVED. This book contains material protected under International and Federal Copyright Laws and Treaties. Any unauthorized reprint or use of this material is prohibited. No part of this book may be reproduced or transmitted in any form or by any means, electronic or mechanical, including photocopying, recording, or by any information storage and retrieval system without express written permission from the author / publisher.

·

ISBN 978-0-9997152-3-9

Dedication

To all the broken people, whether by life's circumstances or God Himself.

To the ones who are in the breaking process, I encourage you to stay the course. The process may seem harsh at times, but you are coming out stronger than you went in.

I especially want to dedicate this book to my grandmother Ruth Agatha Bulze who went home to be with the Lord this year 2019. I will see you in glory when the trump sounds.

Thank You

I must give thanks and praise once again to my Lord and Savior Jesus Christ for allowing me to write yet another book on His behalf. This one was truly a labor of love as it came with many setbacks, but it is finished.

I say thank you to my sister/friend Monique Carridice-Love for her wisdom and constant encouragement to write this book during the times I procrastinated and for her constant prayers.

I cannot forget my leaders Bishop Curt Courtenay and Pastor Aracely Courtenay for all they do to keep this woman grounded because life gets crazy sometimes.

Thank you to all the people God used from my childhood to adulthood to crush my spirit and break my reliance on others. If others never walked away or treated me unkind, the lessons and the wisdom gained from it would never have taken place. The books would not have been written.

Finally, I say thank you to the people who were witnesses to the breaking, pruning, as well as crushing, and offered words of encouragement along the way. Honorable mentions include Issy Francis, Barbara Harvey, Ayesha Reid, Pastor Ivonne Cave.

TABLE OF CONTENTS

Introduction -- 9

Chapter 1 – The World's Cage ------------------------ 13

Chapter 2 – The Zoo – The World ------------------ 17

Chapter 3 – The Barrier and the Spectators---------- 23

Chapter 4 – The Pain of Brokenness ----------------- 29

Chapter 5 – The Fragments of Life ------------------- 41

Chapter 6 – The Clean-up ---------------------------- 49

Chapter 7 – Identity Solidified ----------------------- 53

Chapter 8 – The Great Interruption ----------------- 59

Chapter 9 – The Pruning ----------------------------- 67

Chapter 10 – The Secret of Brokenness -------------- 77

Chapter 11 – It Takes Pressure ---------------------- 83

Chapter 12 – The Truth of Love --------------------- 91

Chapter 13 – Love Is a Servant ---------------------- 97

Chapter 14 – Love Is Bold --------------------------- 105

Chapter 15 – Contagious Love ---------------------- 113

Chapter 16 – The Light of Love --------------------- 125

Chapter 17 – The Power of Love -------------------- 131

Chapter 18 – The Fellowship of Love --------------- 139

Conclusion – The Greatest Commandment ········ 147

Spiritual Inventory ································· 155

Prayer ··· 157

About the Author ·································· 163

Introduction

When we are broken by God, He kills our reliance on others. He must always have first place in our lives. If we are constantly hurt by what others do or say and overwhelmed by life situations, it means we have removed God from His rightful position in our lives and made these things a priority. Consequently, we set ourselves up to be broken by life's challenges.

God always breaks us for a purpose but when life breaks us, we are left feeling rejected. God allows others to betray us, so we can unearth the underlying issues. Their betrayal makes us feel abandoned, but this will only last a moment if we lean on God for His healing touch.

God allowed me to experience betrayal and abandonment by friends for a purpose. I had to understand firsthand what it was to feel pain and be broken in spirit to write about it. I needed to write from a place of experience. You cannot fully express and put into words what you haven't lived through. Actually, you would only be guessing how the other person felt. However, it's an entirely different

Introduction

story when you have journeyed through the same winding and treacherous pathways of life.

Initially, I was hesitant to write this book about brokenness because I thought I would do so from a place of bitterness. However, after indulging in some introspection, I discovered I did not want to write because I was afraid to experience the pain all over again. But I also learned that transparency and feeling the emotions are just tools that equip us to move forward into complete healing. Also, transparency is how I connect with my readers by being open and real.

No one wants to hear or read about how we got over if we cannot talk about the real raw emotions we felt during those dark periods of life. Speaking up about the anger you felt, the sadness, the lonely nights, and rejection lets others know they are not alone in their frame of mind. Our transparency reassures other people they can come out on the opposite side and be made whole.

We often look at other people's lives and figure they always had it together. Or we may look at someone who is at a standstill and figure the person doesn't want anything good in life. We would rather make assumptions than to put in the effort and find out the truth.

I do believe assumptions are the main reasons for all the racial tension in this country. No one wants to do the leg work anymore. It's easier to say divide than it is to work to unify. Thus, we have a broken society trying to fix itself through separation. Unity is always the key, but we will never have true unity without love at the core, specifically, the love of Christ.

The world as we know it will always display the symptoms of brokenness if the Christian community and body of Christ sit idly by and feel no sense of responsibility or burden to do anything.

This love comes with a price, which includes going beyond one's self and stepping into harm's way to change a people and a nation. We are so comfortable within our church walls that we rarely go beyond ourselves to put love on the stage. Jesus' entire ministry was about love and done through the spirit of love. Love is the catalyst of every form of change that has ever taken place in this world. Love is the word most casually thrown around; yet, so few demonstrate its true essence.

What would happen if those Christians who possess the love of God radically step out of the shadows and into the light? What would happen if we stand up to the bully Satan and proclaim Jesus is love and that He died for our sins? I am

Introduction

not talking about merely spitting out words but not applying them to our lives. No! I mean standing on the streets declaring the love of God with a gentle spirit that does not condemn. Each person we encounter daily should walk away feeling loved. Specifically, they should walk away feeling as though they encountered God Himself because they did – through the Holy Spirit living in us.

Take this journey with me. Let's travel through the breaking stages of the Christian voyage as we grow from babes in Christ into mature men and women of God. This journey is seen in the breaking process God allows to take place in us. It is seen in the shaping of the clay by the potter's hand. The journey is seen in the pruning and crushing of our lives as trees and olives in the vineyard of God. When we become mature believers, we will possess the greatest weapon the Holy Spirit wants to reveal in us.

Open your heart and mind to receive and understand what God reveals to you on the pages of this book. I am still on this journey of being broken. Nevertheless, my understanding has shifted. I have completely surrendered to the living, all-powerful God.

Chapter 1
The World's Cage

The world cannot accept him, because it neither sees him nor knows him. But you know him, for he lives with you and will be in you (John 14:17).

The world has been in chaos and a broken state since the fall of Adam and Eve in the garden. The world is also trapped in a cage that is heavily guarded by the prince of darkness. This prince will not give up his hostages without a fight. He has multiple weapons and tactics to defend his domain. Moreover, his loyal minions are just as ruthless as he is when it comes to keeping their prisoners in bondage.

The cage of the world seems impossible to escape when we are in search of a better life in the kingdom of light where God is the King. God is also the Father who longs to receive all His creation into the fold. He wants to rescue them from the grips and the illusions of Satan.

Many people ask if God is the maker of the universe and everything in it why He doesn't forcibly take the world away from Satan. While it is true God created the entire universe including man, it is also true He gave us a free will that allows us to choose. God will not intrude on our ability to choose light or darkness. That's our decision. We must make the choice to leave the world of sin for the life in Jesus Christ.

The world at its present stage is in a broken condition enslaved to a wicked master, the prince of this world. Brokenness in the world is completely different from the brokenness of believers in Christ. Actually, the majority of the world does not know they are broken. They have no idea they are trapped, even though they perceive themselves to be free.

I will try to explain to the best of my ability what God showed me about the world and brokenness. You may ask why I am talking about being broken in the world if this book is for believers. It is significant because to truly understand the breaking process of God as believers of Christ, we need to get a clear picture of the world.

The breaking, pruning, molding, and trials of Christians are directly connected to the world and what God wants to activate in our lives. The following story will give us a glimpse of the world through spiritual eyes, rather than using our natural eyes.

On a bright sunny summer day, a family decided to take their children to the zoo to see the latest addition to the zoo family – a baby lion. A lion hadn't been born at that zoo in a long time, so the public was excited to see the cub. As the family arrived at the zoo and presented the pre-purchased tickets at the gate, the children squealed in excitement. Then they all made their way to the lion's sanctuary because that is why they were there.

The picture of the baby lion cub playing as his mom looked on was fascinating to the audience. The crowd began cheering and calling the cub excitedly never realizing that their excitement was aggravating the momma lion. Momma lion became so annoyed with the intruders that she charged at the crowd of people and ran smack right into the plexiglass barrier that was erected to keep the animals from escaping while protecting the onlookers.

Everyone was startled. All the people shrieked forgetting that the lion could not get to them due to the fence. After the initial shock subsided, they all slowly walked away to see the next exhibit.

This incident will become a distant memory soon enough for the humans involved but for the lion, it's a constant reminder that he is not free. He is nothing more than a conversation piece for the constant stream of visitors who frequent the zoo with each passing year.

While the story above is fictional, it symbolizes the world and the Christian perspective perfectly. The world is the zoo. The kingdom of darkness is the barrier, and you guessed it – the crowd or onlookers are the believers. I know! What? That was the initial expression to this analogy that leaped into my spirit. I sat down and pondered this crazy thought. Eventually, I brushed it off, but God brought it back to my mind during a conversation with a church sister. I started telling her about the caged mentality of the animals in the zoo and immediately, the dots started connecting. I ended my conversation and journaled the thoughts that came so quickly. That started the process of writing this book you are currently reading.

Chapter 2

The Zoo – The World

> In whom the god of this world hath blinded the minds of them which believe not, lest the light of the glorious gospel of Christ, who is the image of God, should shine unto them (2 Corinthians 4:4 KJV).

The world is both blinded and bound by the original sinful nature of Adam and Eve. The Word of God says they are groping in the darkness. In other words, they are desperately trying to find a way to God who gives them freedom. However, they do not realize they are, in fact, searching for God.

People have been trapped for so long that some eventually give up trying. On the other hand, there are hunters and roamers like the lion who do not like to be bound. They will lash out at everything and anyone they consider a threat. The zoo is comprised of many different animal species and various enclosures with different levels of security. Similarly, the world has a set of systems and rules that regulate their behavioral patterns thinking they are free. The Devil has blinded their eyes with a dark veil as was said in our opening scripture.

In the natural zoo, some animals may walk around on the grounds of the compound. They are not dangerous, so they roam freely. While these animals believe they are free, they are not. Their belief does not change the reality that they are encaged. They cannot get past the animal control staff of the zoo. These zookeepers will capture any creature that appears to be getting too close to the exit of the zoo.

Zookeepers are like addictions that keep people trapped in an endless cycle such as substance abuse, whether it is alcohol or illicit drugs. Many celebrities have talked about their struggles with addictions. They described substance abuse as something that draws them backward. It is a lifestyle that is difficult to quit. These addictions have such a strong grip on their lives they will not break free on their own. They need an intervening party or event to help them. Jesus calls this being a slave to sin.

Jesus answered them, "Most assuredly, I say to you, whoever commits sin is a slave of sin" (John 8:34).

The lion represents the next type of people trapped in the zoo or the world. These are the ones who know they are helplessly confined and are angry at folks who live freely. They aggressively charge at the people who laugh and enjoy life but fail to see the barrier between them.

I would compare these people to the atheists, who despite having overwhelming facts about the existence of God refuse to be swayed. Their tireless efforts of trying to prove Christianity wrong keep them blinded to the truth – the barrier, which is the veil of darkness.

A wrong focus will always have us hitting walls. Hence, if the confined would shift their focus from the people to their environment, they would eventually see the barrier. But they are so focused on proving Christians wrong about the existence of God, they cannot see the evidence all points to God.

> For the invisible things of him from the creation of the world are clearly seen, being understood by the things that are made, [even] his eternal power and Godhead; so that they

are without excuse (Romans 1:20).

Finally, in every zoo, there are great escape artists. These "Harry Houdinis" will somehow find a way to escape the zoo completely. They are angry that they are caged, and are desperate for freedom. Their focus is not on the spectators. Rather, their minds are fixated on figuring out the system and devising a way to get out. They are caged physically but not mentally. Think about the gurus in yoga and eastern meditation who train their minds to be deeply focused. That's how they operate. However, this mental freedom is just a mirage. Their freedom is just as limited as the animals who roam the grounds.

Over time, their mental freedom catches the attention of the zookeeper who traps them again. Any level of mental freedom can eventually lead to the truth, and the Enemy knows it. Therefore, he keeps their thoughts on themselves as the enlightened ones. These people believe in God, but they do not want to use the route He has laid out to get to Him.

Just knowing there is a God but ignoring the way to God is fruitless. Consequently, these people are recaptured in the caged system because Jesus is the only way to God.

> Jesus saith unto him, I am the way, the truth, and the life: no man cometh unto the Father, but by me (John 14:6).

There are some who will totally escape the zoo – the world and evade capture. They will live freely in Jesus. The freed people become Christians. However, just because they are free doesn't mean their lives are a bed of roses and fresh sunshine shining on a field of daisies. After a while, the Christians are taken through a crushing, pruning, and breaking process to refine them and expose their true purpose.

Many Christians willingly accept the process, which makes it a short one for them. On the other hand, there are others in the Christian community who become stubborn and refuse to surrender to the process of refinement. Therefore, theirs will be long and difficult. At the end of it all, whether short or long, the will of God must be done.

If you are wondering about the people or animals that get recaptured, here are the facts: some will try to escape again, while others will fall into hopelessness if their efforts to get out seem futile. Eventually, they will give in to their fate of being caged forever. The ones who fall into this state think they are too far gone for God to save them or even love them; these are the backsliders.

The analogy of the zoo is also applicable to believers, but that's not relevant to this book. No matter what type of person is represented in the world, one thing is certain: God doesn't want anyone to die and go to a Christless eternity.

Chapter 3

The Barrier and the Spectators

> But if our gospel be hid, it is hid to them that are lost (2 Corinthians 4:3).

In the previous chapter, we talked about the various types of people in the world and their perception of the environment they reside in. Now, we will focus on both the barrier and the spectators because they overlap. The kingdom of darkness is like a large veil covering the eyes of the unsaved from seeing the truth of God, as well as His love and grace for humanity. God did not come to condemn the world but that the world through Him – Jesus – might be saved (John 3:17).

> And if our gospel be hid; it is only hid to those who are lost: in whom the god of this world hath blinded the minds of them which believe not lest the light of the glorious gospel

of Christ, who is the image of God, should shine upon them. (2 Corinthians 4:3-4 KJV)

The world is blinded because Satan has closed people's minds to the things of God. No person who encounters Christ will remain unchanged. The Enemy knows this and makes every effort to keep the veil of darkness intact.

When Jesus was here on the earth, He tried to get the people to see the truth about their human condition. He invited them to be exposed to the light – Jesus. However, mankind loves darkness rather than light because their actions are evil (John 3:19). These evil deeds are the result of sin in the flesh due to the fall in the garden of Eden.

A barrier is a structure that is erected to either keep something in or something out. It is used as a security measure or safety net depending on its purpose. The unsaved may have all kinds of issues going on that keep them from drawing close to God. However, many times when they uncover their veils and try to remove the issues, they are discouraged by insensitive Christians who judge and condemn them. As a consequence, they retreat further into darkness.

I wonder how many times our bickering with and laughing at each other, as well as our judgment of the lost, have caused them to resent and reject God. Christians are not the only reason the lost cannot see the light, but I must confess, we contribute to the problem by unknowingly putting their dark veil back on.

How? You may ask. Simple! Our judgment is like the spectators in the analogy pointing out to the groundskeeper the weaknesses in his barrier. He, Satan, then makes the veil stronger and gains a tighter grip on his prisoners. For example, a gay person walks into a church for the first time because he is curious; a prostitute walks into the church half-naked or a known HIV infected person sits next to you at work in the lunchroom. All three of these characters were drawn to you, the Christian or to the church building.

The Holy Spirit drew them close to the fence, which triggered a secret switch that can remove the veil. Just as the door was about to open, the insensitive Christian commented about the gay individual and the prostitute who walked into the church building. The HIV infected individual was physically scorned by the professing believer. All three persons experienced some form of judgment and snapped. They step away from the secret switch – the very thing that drew them. The cunning Devil observing every moment and action disables the secret switch.

God is very rich in His mercy, and He knows where all the secret switches are that will remove the veils. He just needs the lost to come close enough to the fence once more for the Holy Spirit to release the button and set the captives free.

The people in the world are curious about the church, but they are also cautious and skeptical of sincere believers. This is so because they are constantly rejected and labeled as hopeless by people who are supposed to light the way to the kingdom of God. I urge you to be conscious of your interaction with the unsaved. I am not saying to agree with their sins or refrain from telling them the truth of the Word of God. I am saying to reflect on your way of thinking when you were in that condition bound by sin and darkness.

Sometimes, those who grew up in the church and got saved at a young age find it difficult to avoid this way of thinking. But remember the Word says, "All have sinned and fallen short of the glory of God" Romans 8:28 (KJV). We are also told that our righteousness is like filthy rags (Isaiah 64:6).

Balancing our approach to sin with the Word of God may present a challenge, but that's where the Holy Spirit comes into the picture. He is the one who convicts and changes the hearts of men and women. He is the one who leads us into all truth. He is the one who rebukes, reproves, and corrects. He is our counselor here on the earth. He is the one who lights the way in the darkness. He is our helper and so much more. We must speak the truth, but our approach must be done in all wisdom.

Now that we have established the world is broken due to the sin nature inherited from Adam and Eve, we will examine two important aspects of the breaking stages of a Christian:

1. Why it is necessary to go through trials
2. Why it is important to allow God to work on us

The crushing of our wills to conform and align with the will of God is uncomfortable. Some days, you will want to throw in the towel in defeat. While this stage is difficult, God is gracious and patient. He even gives us comfort in crushing.

Action Step: Here is where we ask the Holy Spirit to work through and in us to fulfill God's purpose on the earth. This journey of brokenness taught me that the spirit must be the leader in everything we do on this earth. If we do not allow Him to be the authority in our lives, it means we are openly rebellious. Do you remember what happened when Satan rebelled against God? He was cast down from heaven and lost his glory. Thank God for his amazing grace and mercy in our lives when we rebel.

Chapter 4

The Pain of Brokenness

He heals the brokenhearted and binds up their wounds (Psalm 147:3).

This verse clearly shows us that brokenness and pain are associated. Anything that is wounded will experience some type of pain. The verse also tells us that God will heal our hurts and bandage our wounds. I read the verse, and I asked myself the question: how can someone in a broken state write about the topic of brokenness? I am not an expert like some of the greats who have written on being broken, but I do know the terrible feeling it brings. I know the agony of being crushed in body, mind, and spirit.

In your broken state, your emotions are all over the place. Sometimes it seems as if you have no control over the tears that gush out. The things you fear the most taunt you and refuse to budge no matter how hard you try to ignore them. In our broken places, we come face-to-face with the residue of darkness in our lives.

When unsaved people come face-to-face with their darkness, they may contemplate suicide as the only way of escape. Whether we are saved or unsaved, we all have an encounter with the darkness in us.

Currently, I am looking at a cold half-filled cup of peppermint tea, and I imagine my cup falling to the ground. What would be the result? I will lose my favorite cup, spill my tea, and have broken pieces littered on the floor. As a casual observer, I would see the shattered pieces scattered all over the place. Some would be big and very visible; however, others would be tiny specks that are barely visible. Yet, these are the very pieces that would do me the most harm if I accidentally stepped on them.

Seeing the mess and knowing the dangers, I sigh, get a broom, as well as a dustpan, and proceed to sweep the floor. I would be very careful to remove those dangerous, tiny particles to prevent future pain. Furthermore, I would empty the contents of the dustpan (a mixture of broken glass and dust) into the trash can. Afterward, I would walk away and that would be the end of the story. That cup would be forgotten and replaced by a new cup.

On the other hand, if the cup had thoughts and feelings that could be expressed, how would the cup define those feelings? What words would the cup use to voice those feelings so we could understand given the fact that it is an inanimate object that has no feelings? I want you to stretch your imagination for a minute. Imagine yourself as someone's favorite cup, the one she uses quite often to pour her drink of choice. Sometimes the contents are warm or cool and other times, they are piping hot, but you can handle it. You were made to handle any content that is poured into you. You proudly keep the contents of whatever liquid you are given to its correct temperature for any length of time.

Hold that picture in your head. Can you sense the feelings of accomplishment the cup has whenever it is chosen and used instead of the others on the shelf? Can you relate to the excitement of this mug as it is taken from the kitchen cabinet time after time? Can you feel the contents of hot chocolate or the heated, cooling sensation of the peppermint tea that is poured into its bosom time after time?

Now, imagine you are that very cup. One day, as usual, you are excited to have been chosen, but all of a sudden, you find yourself abruptly falling. You're screaming for dear life as your body comes into contact with the ground with a loud crashing sound. The impact of the fall sends a searing pain through your genetic make-up. Like a puzzle, you feel your parts separating, but there is nothing you can do about it. This is the feeling of brokenness. Brokenness will make us think we are about to die. Job said: "My spirit is broken, my days are extinguished, the grave is ready for me" (Job 17:1).

The crash scattered parts of a vessel that was once whole all over the room. Things will never be the same again. Some fragments went under the table; some went under the stove, while others fell between the cracks of a tiled kitchen floor. Yet, there are others in plain sight albeit, imperceptible to the naked eye. The things no one sees can still do damage when they come into contact with exposed flesh or in this case, another human life.

Your life has been shattered. You look at your fragmented and scattered pieces over the vast expanse of the kitchen and accept nothing can make you whole again – it seems. On one side of the great divide is your heart; on another side are your emotions. Further back are the dismembered parts of what gives you your sense of self. This tragedy has fallen upon your life, and you are left wondering: who am I now that I am broken? What will become of me and my fragmented parts? What will life be like in the trash – the dump? Is my life salvageable? These are the haunting questions that can plague the lives of believers when we come to the realization that we are broken. The broken pieces of life are constant reminders that life happened.

The owner of the cup gathers the pieces of the vessel by sweeping the floor and proceeds to place the fragments into the garbage. However, unlike this cup, our spiritual lives as vessels are always salvageable. Why? Because our owner is the ultimate Potter who is the expert at mending all broken vessels.

> The LORD is near to the brokenhearted And, saves those who are crushed in spirit (Psalm 34:18).

This is the greatest of all hope to anyone living in this world. Whether we are believers or not, God promised to mend us when we surrender our brokenness to Him. Many people are walking around believing they are whole, but the truth is they are very fragmented. Many know their lives are broken but are at a loss because they don't know there is someone who can mend them.

God desires to mend our lives and make us into vessels He can fill. The psalmist David asked God to fill his cup, and over in the gospels, Jesus told the woman at the well to drink from His living water. The same should be said of our lives today. We can become fillable vessels to be used by God in the lives of others. We can do so when we avail ourselves to Him and let Him work on our vessels – our lives. We often try to fix our dismantled situations for ourselves but in doing so we make an even bigger mess of our lives.

Our lives are the vessels God uses to reach others. He is constantly shaping us to conform to His will for us. This shaping comes in many forms but it always comes with discomfort or pain. The severity of the discomfort we experience during this shaping process depends on how pliable our lives are while on the potter's wheel.

We are the clay in the hands of an amazing Potter. The pieces that have been shattered and scattered due to abandonment from family and friends can be found and fixed in the hands of the Master.

Naturally speaking, some clay is hard due to exposure to the air. The moisture within the clay is dried out from exposure. Many people's hearts become hardened when they experience hurt. This hurt, if left unchecked, becomes bitterness and self-hatred. It has even caused some to take on other personalities as a defense mechanism. Clay that has become hardened needs extra molding and folding with the water of the Word, which is the Holy Spirit. Naturally speaking, a potter sprinkles water onto hardened clay. He gently folds the clay over and over adding water a little at a time. Too much water on the clay will make it like soup and then it is not moldable.

When the Spirit invades our hearts, He hits us with hard truths about ourselves. The Holy Spirit reveals the truth about our condition a little at a time. Again, too much water in the clay creates a soup-like texture; likewise, too much revelation about ourselves at once weakens our souls. When the soul of a new believer is weakened, he is more vulnerable to attacks from the Enemy. Therefore, the Holy Spirit reveals truth and works on us in stages just like a potter.

Every time we are confronted and convicted by the Word of God, we become a little softer in the hands of God and easily allow ourselves to be shaped. On the other hand, when we resist, the shaping process is prolonged, and we experience severe pain instead of discomfort because of our stubborn wills.

God desires to fill us with all the fullness of Himself. It may seem impossible to be filled with all the fullness of God. Yet, that is exactly what He wants to do in us.

> That he would grant you, according to the riches of his glory, to be strengthened with might by his Spirit in the inner man;

> 17 That Christ may dwell in your hearts by faith; that ye, being rooted and grounded in love,
>
> 18 May be able to comprehend with all saints what is the breadth, and length, and depth, and height;
>
> 19 And to know the love of Christ, which passeth knowledge, that ye might be filled with all the fulness of God (Ephesians 3:16-19).

What is the fullness of God? Well the above-mentioned scriptures let us know exactly what that is. It is love. God is love. The very essence and genetic makeup of God is love. Everything we know about God will always lead us back to one singular thought and action, which is love. Human beings were created out of love; hence, we can understand why we are always searching for love, even in the wrong places, things, and people at times. We desire to be loved because we were created in the image of God, for God is love.

This initial part of us was somehow lost when mankind fell way back in the garden of Eden when everything was perfect. A small measure of love still exists in our hearts. God desires to take us back to the pre-fallen state where love is all we knew and lived. We can now get an idea of the scripture that says, "until Christ be formed in you." Christ did everything out of love, and He told us He only did what He saw His Father do.

Lives filled and running over with the love of God, are effective in His kingdom. We will no longer be seen, but the Christ in us will be portrayed at all times. Ultimately, when this world sees Christ in us, they will see the Father as well. Jesus said anyone who has seen Him has seen the Father, and they will know that "I and my Father are one." Our lives put Jesus on display, and Jesus reveals the Father. Consequently, all of creation will know that God loves and He is love. Love can eradicate the deepest darkness.

The presence of love eradicates fear. Love is light; love is the Way, the Truth, and the Life. Love is the Creator. Our mere words can never give language to all the things that love is. To do so would mean we can describe God in His entirety; God is unsearchable and indescribable.

Christ is continually being formed in us as we journey through life. Eventually, we will experience the height, length, breadth, and depth of God's love. My prayer is that believers in Christ would once again represent the children's song that says:

> Love is a flag flown high in the castle of my heart, in the castle of my heart, in the castle of my heart
> So, fly it high in the sky let the whole world, let the whole world know, let the whole world know
> That the king is the resident there.
>
> Author Unknown

Today's generation no longer wants to sing the hymns because they seem boring. I can understand the sentiments. However, the hymns are packed with the power experienced by the writers who tell their stories in song. If you understand that, you will appreciate the words that make up some of the greatest hymns ever.

The love of God was so formed in the lives of these writers nothing could destroy their faith and belief in Him. Though their faith was shaken and tested at times, they stood firm in the midst of adversity. They clung to their hope in God and the truth that God is who He says He is.

The love of God will empower you to withstand the greatest test, even in the face of death. Believers in the first-century church were willing to give up their lives for God because they understood the power and message of the cross. They understood all the cross stood for, and they gladly gave up their lives for it.

It would seem as if the times we are currently living in are gradually taking us back to the days of the first-century church. It appears as if believers in Christ will once again have to become martyrs for Christ. Thousands of Christians in other parts of the world are already being persecuted for their belief in the God of the Bible. In the western world, we take the cost of the cross for granted, and we often neglect our inner witness to the point of our flames being extinguished.

It is because of the mercies of God that we are not consumed when we fail to uphold our confession of faith in the Lord Jesus Christ. May our lives once again portray the God of the Bible that will draw the lost to the light of Christ inside us. May we experience the passion of the Christ in our hearts in a new way to fan the flames of our inner witness. That way, we can be the image of God on the earth, the image of love.

Here is where I am asking you to do something radical and seemingly unnecessary. You may think it doesn't take all of what I ask. But sometimes, it's the crazy things that revitalize our lives and change us for the better.

The Challenge

For the next 30 or 31 days, I want you to disconnect from everything. I want you to just read the Bible and

Christian books, as well as listen to preaching and Christian music. That means you can't open any of your current social media platforms for the entire month. Every time you feel the urge to do something that is a distraction, pick up the Bible and read. The objective is to saturate your life for an entire month with the Word of God. Document your thoughts and struggles with this challenge as the days go by. At the end of the month, refer to the beginning of the challenge and evaluate your state of mind.

1. Is there a difference in your life?
2. What is the biggest obstacle you encountered on the challenge?
3. Did you overcome the obstacle or did you give in?
4. Did God speak to you during the month?
5. If He did, in what ways did He speak to you?
6. What is your biggest take away from the challenge?

The month is going to seem as if it is dragging its foot but hang in there. Take one day at a time. Try to communicate with God in prayer as much as possible and enjoy the process. It's not hard to do, and it's not torture! You're an overcomer. You got this! I believe in you.

Chapter 5

The Fragments of Life

Heal me, O LORD, and I shall be healed; save me, and I shall be saved: for thou art my praise (Jeremiah 17:14).

Do you recall in our previous chapters the shattered cup and the fragments that littered different sections of the kitchen floor? These fragments represent the various parts of us we have given away or that were taken away. Consequently, we no longer know who we are because the only view in sight is a memory of who we used to be. Our view is a sharp, rough exterior where pieces fell off, with an interior combination of fear and hope. We have the hope of becoming whole again while fear and mistrust – our teachers – taught us life will always be the same.

We became fragments because we gave so much of ourselves to others who didn't value the treasure we carried.

Furthermore, we didn't have any self-worth and sold our value cheaply for friendships, husbands, wives, jobs, validation, and so forth. With so much of our lives in the hands of others we got lost. Today, we search aimlessly and in vain because we cannot remember where those pieces are.

Jesus is the only one who can locate all the pieces of our hearts that fell in between the cracks. He says, "Come to me all who are heavy burdened, and I will give you rest" (Matthew 11:28). The Lord is with those who are heartbroken and discouraged, and He gives hope (Psalm 34:28).

It does not matter if you found *almost* all the pieces of the cup and glued it back together, without every piece, the cup will never be whole. There will always be a visible sign of something missing. Depending on where the missing piece came from that cup may never be able to hold anything. Certainly, it will never function at its maximum capacity without that one piece. It will forever be a leaking vessel.

This cup and the damage done are true representations of our lives. We try to fill the missing areas in with things that bring us no fulfilment. Getting a better job, making more money, becoming popular with everyone; yet, we are empty inside. We can travel anywhere in the world, buy anything we want, wear the clothes we desire, but deep down inside, we are still not content. No matter how many times we try to put our lives together using temporal things to cover the brokenness, we will forever have fractures and miss important parts of our genetic makeup.

The more God tries to pour into us, the more we leak because we are broken. We have not surrendered to His sovereign will so we can be completely whole. God wants to mend our shattered lives and replace the missing parts of us.

God is the missing link in our lives. Choosing to hide our hurts, disappointments, frustrations, anger, bitterness, and everything we think makes us unworthy hinders the work of God in our lives. It prevents Him from being the gap filler that will keep us from leaking all our issues onto unsuspecting individuals who cross our paths daily.

How do we know when we are leaking? Our speech always tells us. We speak negative words of doubt and fear and accept mediocrity when we say, "It's just the way I am." Words like these hold prominent places in our lives. Moreover, we constantly seek approval and validation from people who don't even like us.

You may be a fragmented mess right now, but you don't have to remain that way forever. Quit trying to find your scattered pieces and turn to God with what you have. If you do so, you will discover that God already has the missing parts in His possession. He eagerly waits to remake us into vessels better than we were before. He is the Creator of all things. Therefore, He knows how to mend and create new parts.

No matter how hard we fight to put the pieces of our lives back together, we will never succeed. The more we struggle to fix ourselves the more damage we inflict on others. It's a vicious cycle because broken things cause major harm, even though it's never intentional.

It must be a sad sight in the eyes of God when He looks at broken people accusing each other and pointing out each other's faults. They are all fragmented. Broken people can't help but see the brokenness of others. While they may be able to identify other broken people, they can never help them. Chaos often takes place when one hurt person tries to help another hurt individual. It takes a person who was broken but has been mended to point the wounded person to Christ to get healing and wholeness.

When Christ makes us whole, we can empathize with those who walk around wounded with hurt and pain. We understand how difficult it is to identify ourselves as fragmented. We know in that condition, we don't see clearly. We have a distorted view that we are whole when, in fact, we are messed up. Sadly, people who have been made whole walk around afraid of the wounded. They are scared that getting too close will cause them to get scarred again. If Christ has made you whole, don't be afraid to reach out to the broken people of this world. Our only job is to point the way to Jesus who heals. We lead hurting people to Christ by loving them. In fact, we ought to love people even when they push us away. Don't give up on the wounded. You were once in their position – hopeless and with a skewed perspective.

I know how it feels to be pushed away and rejected by others when I was hurting on the inside. Hurt people find it difficult to ask for help. They don't want to burden others with their issues, so they often isolate themselves from the world. The worst thing the loved ones of those who are hurting can do is to let them remain in isolation. This will only compound the problem. Therefore, you must push past their defenses with love and genuine concern. Love is the key to breaking down the walls hurting people set up to protect themselves. A warm hug, bright smile and a sincere "How are you doing?" will open a door for the hurting to welcome you into their world.

The only way to approach those who hurt is with love. We cannot pick and choose who deserves to be shown love. Unfortunately, many in the body of Christ are being very selective about whom they will extend love to. Inevitably, this creates a warped view of love.

Everything that is currently shattered in our lives can be made whole once it meets the love of God. Broken lives are His specialty. He takes those jagged pieces and remakes them. Some people may be left with one or two scars to show the beauty of brokenness. Others are made completely brand new to show the greatness of God's work.

It's not for us to decide who will be made brand new or who will be put back together with the broken pieces. God heals, mends and remakes us according to His plans and purposes for our lives. One thing is guaranteed, Jesus lovingly works on all who encounter Him.

This world scorns broken things. They see them as useless and something to be discarded. However, God sees value in the very things man regards as trash. The only things God sees as trash are the stumbling blocks in our lives that prevent us from reflecting His glory: holding grudges, jealousy, pride, bitterness, stubbornness, fear, control, and the list can go on. Brokenness blemishes our personalities and makes them unattractive. Is it any wonder one broken person often scorns another person in the same condition? No one who is broken sees correctly. We become suspicious of each other because we cannot see the full picture of the people around us.

Have you ever taken a piece of broken glass and tried to look through it? Depending on the thickness of the glass, the view will be very blurry. It's the same for us as human beings. The depth of life's experiences that shaped us and then broke us will determine our views of others.

It's easy to walk away from people without a second thought because others did the same to us. This is a tell-tale sign of being hurt by life. However, when we come into contact with Jesus, we will no longer be able to walk away from people who are hurting. We will recognize the symptoms and approach those people in love. Please note, I am not saying you should try to fix a hurting person. We cannot do so; only Jesus can. Loving and fixing are two different things. We are the hands and feet of Jesus on the earth extending love to those who hurt.

Chapter 6

The Clean-up

> He saved us, not on the basis of deeds which we have done in righteousness, but according to His mercy, by the washing of regeneration and renewing by the Holy Spirit (Titus 3:5).

The process of being cleaned up is very hard to endure. You are pushed and pulled in many different directions. It does not feel good and quite frankly, it is embarrassing because spectators are looking at you. While the Master is picking up the pieces left behind in the cracks because of the fall, many onlookers stand at the sidelines witnessing what God is doing to pull you out of your mess.

We may feel a measure of discomfort and shame when our faults are exposed and others realize we are not as perfect as we pretend to be. Nevertheless, it is a blessing because the same people who see you in your ruins will also witness what God does in your life after He has cleansed and remade you into something beautiful. God puts us on a stage for everyone to see the process and the results. This stage is when we are on the potter's wheel. There, others get to see the Master pounding us back into shape or creating a totally different vessel.

The cleanup stage begins with us seeing the truth about our lives – we are broken. Many of us refuse to acknowledge the fact that our lives have fallen apart for one reason or another. The longer we stay in denial, the longer it will take us to heal. Admitting we are in a bad condition is crucial. It is the beginning stage of the process. We are closer to letting God work on our lives.

Wholeness can only be achieved when we let God deal with the things in us that are evidence of us coming from the kingdom of darkness. In the book of Colossians, it says we have been transported from the darkness to the kingdom of Jesus.

> Who hath delivered us from the power of darkness, and hath translated us into the kingdom of his dear Son (Colossians 1:13).

In the world of darkness, we defined who we were based on what the world said. True to form, the world distorted our values from what God originally designed them to be on the earth. Hence, we were contaminated beings full of the world's ideals. But the light of Christ now illuminates everything in us that was hidden because of the veil of darkness. We cannot live in God's kingdom with the mindset we currently possess. It is a way of thinking derived from being born into the kingdom of darkness.

Now that we are no longer in the kingdom of darkness, but children of light, our lives must reflect the kingdom of God's Son. For this reason, God starts the pruning process after we have walked with Him long enough to have our roots established in Him. He starts the clipping and cutting when we have grown to the stage in Him where we produce branches that would soon bear fruit.

A farmer does not prune a plant that has just burst forth from the ground. The pruning process begins when the plant is strong enough to withstand the cutting and the shaping of the shears. This action is not designed to kill the plant, but to let the plant flourish correctly and produce an abundant harvest. A plant that is not pruned will bring forth a small harvest or no crop at all.

Chapter 7
Identity Solidified

> Yet to all who did receive him, to those who believed in his name, he gave the right to become children of God (John 12:12).

> You did not choose me, but I chose you and appointed you so that you might go and bear fruit—fruit that will last—and so that whatever you ask in my name the Father will give you (John 15:16).

When God is ready to prune us, He first establishes our identity in Him. After that, He turns the mirror to us so we can see ourselves just as we are in an unrefined state.

It is important that we are confident in who we are in God before any cutting can take place. Why is this so? If God does not solidify our identity as His children before starting the pruning process, we will immediately think He doesn't love us. Clipping and cutting is painful; hence, we attribute the pain in our lives to His lack of care and love for us. However, this is the opposite of the truth. God allows pain in our lives because:

1. It is a part of the growing process
2. It is a necessary nutrient for the seed of love that is on the inside of every Christian

Establishing our identity in God through Christ will let us know if we are portraying the character of Christ as we should. The word "identity" in the dictionary means oneness and exactness. This means we must look the same; we must act the same, and we must talk the same as Christ.

One reason why we fail to solidify our identity in Christ is the "you factor," which is rebellious and prideful. The "you factor" is a kingdom all by itself. It loves calling the shots. Therefore, giving God control is something most people don't do very easily. I get it. I consider myself as stubborn as they come, but I have come to see this is a manifestation of pride. The Bible says pride goes before a fall.

We must ask ourselves whether we are displaying the nature of Christ in our everyday walk. Are we Christlike all the time or just some of the time? Our identity in Christ is wrapped up in one-word – love. God is love; love is God. It's His name and His character. We cannot separate God from His character. In the Hebrew culture, your family name is worth everything. We seldom see Jewish children on the streets behaving in a manner that is unbefitting to their family name. Why is this? It's because their behavior is a reflection of their parents.

It all makes so much sense to me now. Growing up, whenever I met someone who knew my family, they would always give the highest compliments about them being wonderful. Even though I wasn't intentionally trying to live up to my family name, I exhibited certain qualities because I learned them from my relatives' interactions with each other. As Christians, when we fail to exhibit the character and name of God, we are basically shaming our heavenly family name. 1 Timothy Chapter 6 tells us some traits we must put on as the children of God:

> But, as for you, O man of God, flee these things. Pursue righteousness, godliness, faith, love, steadfastness, gentleness (1 Timothy 6:11 ESV).

The Word of God identifies us as new creations who have been transferred from the kingdom of darkness into the kingdom of light. With this transfer came a new name, which is attached to Jesus. I present to you that as Christians, every time we do anything that is not Christ like we damage our family name. Our reputation as children of God becomes watered down and trashy in the eyes of the world. If we do not understand love, we will always be disconnected from our identity.

> So now faith, hope, and love abide, these three; but the greatest of these is love (1 Corinthians 13:13 ESV).

Look into the internal mirror and ask yourself a question: "Am I showcasing my family qualities?" Think about your earthly family and your interactions with each other. Is it a good relationship or a hostile one? Is your earthly family filled with toxicity or is it Pleasantville? We may have qualities of our earthly family that are undesirable by God's standards. Given that, we must shift our thoughts to those of Christ because we are now a part of a totally different family. We have been adopted into the family of God and as such, the rules and regulations of our previous earthly family are no longer applicable to our lives.

> For through him we both have access by one Spirit unto the Father

> Now therefore ye are no more strangers and foreigners, but fellow citizens with the saints, and of the household of God (Ephesians 2:18-19).

Your family may be known for being quarrelsome, petty, and messy. Nevertheless, you don't have to be that way. You can choose to live as an earthling or as an ambassador for Christ on assignment on the earth. He adopted you and gave you a new name with new characteristics based on who He is and what His name means. His name carries power and authority. It carries supernatural capabilities to transform all of humanity.

God needs His children to align with Him. We are kingdom people looking at the pig slops of this world as if they are delicacies. They are just left-over garbage discarded by the Enemy, garbage he feeds to his captives, the poor lost souls.

When we refuse to let love transform and use us, we are saying God Himself is not powerful enough to change us. How sad it must be for God whenever He hears His children saying they don't have the *agape* form of love. It is ridiculous to believe that God, who created all things, who holds the universe in His hands yet lives inside of us left His very nature outside of us. If this is possible then God is not all-encompassing as His Word says. It means God has limits. If God is limited, then He is just like the Enemy. And if God is like the Enemy, it means at any point in time, the Enemy can defeat God.

Do we believe that? Let us mature in our understanding of love and the God of love. Stop fighting to do your own thing. Instead, surrender to God. Surrendering is a continuous process. Although we surrendered our lives to God to be forgiven of sin, that "you factor" also known as the will needs to be transferred into God's hands. I know it's difficult to hand over the control of ourselves to someone we cannot see. I admit I still struggle with that. However, we have a comrade in Paul. Paul said I die daily, and I beat my flesh into submission to the things of God. Our minds need to be constantly renewed so we can walk boldly in our identity. It can be done. It must be done. And it will be done through our submission to God's leading and Lordship.

Chapter 8
The Great Interruption

> For if you are living according to the [impulses of the] flesh, you are going to die. But if [you are living] by the [power of the Holy] Spirit you are *habitually* putting to death the *sinful* deeds of the body, you will [really] live *forever* (Romans 8: 13 - AMP).

I often ask myself what is the point of submitting to God if it's just going to lead to more pain as He kills our reliance on self and others. With every trial He allows us to walk through, He strips away our pride and the things that would cause us to become gods in our own eyes. This stripping away feels more like a crushing. It can be so painful we often believe we cannot make it through alive. The truth is we will not make it out alive or unchanged. The person we were before entering the process will die. The person God desires will come out stronger and better than the stubborn, prideful individual who went through the crushing, pruning or brokenness.

The pruning and crushing of the believer are two different stages that we must walk through. However, they often feel like the same thing because of the pain we experience during these phases. Each of these stages is needed for the final product to be seen in our lives. The pruning season is where God kills our reliance on outside factors so we can totally depend on Him. The cutting away of our support systems often leaves us naked and exposed to the elements. Some of my support systems include family and friends, job security, and validation. The first of these support systems taken away from me was my friendships.

One day, during my devotional time, God asked me a question: do you love me enough to walk away from your friends? This one hit me hard. In my previous book, I spoke about not having friends when I was growing up, so as an adult when I found a group that I called friends I cherished it. Hence, when God asked me to do such a hard thing, I froze. I didn't have an Abraham moment. I did not agree with God in complete surrender. Nope! I had a typical Orencia aka Rency moment. I dug my heels in, lifted my head in defiance and carried on my merry way.

God will let you have your way – to a point. I say to a point because God will do what He must to accomplish His purpose in your life. He will take His position as your Father and take away what you refuse to give up willingly. The Holy Spirit may be a gentleman but God the Father is like any earthly parent. He makes the hard decisions we choose not to make.

I will never know if that question was a test or not because I didn't obey. However, one day, I looked up and our little group was no more. Friction arose over simple things that should have never been issues.

God also cuts away the dead things that block the roots' nutrients from reaching the other parts of our branches. Cutting is a necessary step that takes place once we decide to deny ourselves and submit to whatever God requires. Sometimes after a plant has been pruned, it may not grow or flourish the way the farmer wanted. This can happen because the plant does not have enough soil at its roots. Consequently, the farmer has to add soil to it. In other instances, the plant may have been pruned too much. An expert farmer will know how to tackle this situation.

In our spiritual lives, we often encounter our stagnant or non-growing stage because of something called the great interruption. The harvest of our lives will never come into fruition if we do not deny ourselves, take up our crosses, and follow in Christ's footsteps.

Somewhere between denying yourself and taking up your cross, the Enemy of the Christ in you can cause an interruption. This great interceptor is the flesh that doesn't want to die. As a result, it goes to great lengths to prevent its death. We have lived in this fleshly state for so long that it doesn't take much for the flesh to talk its way out of being crucified. The flesh will say:

- It doesn't take all that to live for Jesus; you are being too radical
- You are looking and sounding spooky with all this talk about Christ
- Do you really have to read your Bible for that length of time?
- You need a life
- So, are you going to cut that person off just like that?
- She is a Christian too. Do you think you're better than her?

The flesh plays on our weaknesses and insecurities encouraging us to take back our wills. In turn, we stop denying ourselves and become convinced this life is all about us and our happiness. We are so wrapped up in gratifying the flesh that we settle for less. We would rather be miserable with someone who is clearly not for us than be alone for a season. We compromise on the things of God, so we won't be viewed as the Debbie Downer – or party pooper.

The Christian life is not about God making us happy; as a matter of fact, this walk is all about taking up our crosses and following Christ. The cross is heavy but if Jesus carried His cross then we are more than equipped to carry ours. When we deny ourselves, it gives us the strength to carry the cross we are called to bear.

The flesh will always try to convince us to be stubborn and full of pride, so we will not deny ourselves and take up our crosses. The Devil knows the minute we start taking up our crosses, it's all downhill for him. He knows after that the next step for us is being true followers of Christ. A true follower of Christ is a fruit-producing saint. The fruit of our lives can be seen by displaying the nine attributes of the Spirit listed in Galatians. The fruit of the Spirit in the life of a believer is also about making disciples for Christ by winning souls. Sold out believers and followers of Christ willingly and gladly welcome being ostracized for their beliefs. They are radical and follow Christ blindly without question.

Self will keep us from fully surrendering to God. Our reliance on our own abilities and strengths often causes us to become stagnant in the first place. We cannot do anything on our own and think we will become fruitful in Christ.

> Abide in Me, and I in you. As the branch cannot bear fruit of itself, unless it abides in the vine, neither can you, unless you abide in Me (John 15:4).

We need to always abide in Christ because on our own, we cannot produce. We fool ourselves into believing we are the ones in charge when we are not. Self keeps our hearts puffed up with pride, too stubborn to see we are about to self-destruct.

Brokenness prepares us for our purpose and destiny in Christ. It takes us to a place in God that allows us to walk in power and authority. This brokenness comes by the hand of God Himself. He allows the breaking to produce His anointing. This brokenness also kills the pride in our lives, so we won't ever take the glory of God for ourselves.

Brokenness reminds us of our place in God and our humanity thereby keeping us in a place of humility. The second we act as if we can handle life on our own, we are met with another cycle of brokenness where we must deny ourselves all over again. With each cycle, a different level of

Christ is revealed in us. All things work together for the good of those who are called according to His purpose. This includes all of life's trials and every broken cycle we must walk through.

I do not know what phase you are currently in, whether you are a plant that is being pruned or a plant that has stopped growing. Maybe you are a fruit like the olives. God is crushing you to bring you to another level of your awesome self that you have no idea exists. It does not matter the phase you are currently in. What is important is that you recognize where you are and submit your life to the obedience of Christ.

If you have stopped growing, it is time to let God dig the soil around your roots so more nutrients can begin to flow your way. Confess your lukewarm and stagnant attitude to Christ and allow Him to nourish you once more.

We have been in this wrestling match with God for far too long. It is time to completely surrender to His Lordship in our lives. I cannot tell you the many times when I figured God was moving a bit too slowly for my liking. So I took situations into my own hands and refused to surrender everything to Him. However, our Father is so loving that he swooped down and fixed the mess I created. And do you know what my response to Him was? I turned around and did the same thing again – sometimes even worse than before.

Stagnation is the price we pay for refusing to submit. Cycles are repeated when we fail to see the error of our ways. I have been through countless cycles because of my stubborn will and a blurred vision of my situation. But I am forever grateful God didn't cast me aside. He dug up the shallow root system and transplanted me into a richer and deeper soil where I finally started growing again.

God does not wish for anyone to perish, so He takes great care in crushing and pruning us His offspring. Then He sends us into this world with a secret weapon – His light to guide. Some days, you will feel like quitting the process by giving in to your emotions but stay the course. The process only seems long when we are focused on the pain. Fix your eyes on Jesus, and the cutting will seem like nothing. The pruning, crushing, and the brokenness will be worth it when we are on the other side of the pain, which has purpose and destiny wrapped up in one package.

Chapter 9

The Pruning

> Every branch in Me that does not bear fruit, He takes away; and every branch that bears fruit, He prunes it so that it may bear more fruit (John 15:2).

There are three basic types of pruning a farmer may put a tree through for it to grow and bloom beautifully.

The Thinning Process

The thinning process involves removing inner branches and limbs. This allows more air and sunlight to hit the tree letting it get more nutrients for it to grow taller.

We need to get rid of many things in our lives as Christians. James talks about the gossiping and the slandering of each other. Colossians talks about the filthy communications that proceed out of our mouths. Are you still laughing and indulging in the dirty jokes? Are you still using words that are not befitting of you as a child of God on a daily basis? Are you still hanging out with the folks who keep you tied to your past life? It is one thing to hang out with our unsaved family and friends, but we should not indulge in the things they do that bring shame and disgrace to the Father.

When we fully immerse ourselves in immoral behaviors, we are telling the unsaved and unchurched that it's no big deal living this Christian life. Jesus ate and socialized with sinners; this is true, but nowhere in Scripture can we find Jesus behaving in a manner that put His Father to shame.

Christ wants us to be the salt and the light of the world, the changing agent in the darkness. We can't change something that looks so much like our characters. We must be the type of people who are truly separated from the kingdom of darkness. Please, don't confuse being in the world with being a part of the world. Many Christians have this confused. We do not have to compromise our standards to win this world for God. We must interact with the lost but remain unspotted and spoiled by all this world has to offer. The things this world offers are still temporal. They are not essential for living the life of a kingdom citizen.

In the book of Romans, Paul tells us not to be conformed to this world's standards, but be renewed in our minds (Romans 12:2). This renewing of the mind involves leaving behind the customs of this world such as are mentioned in Colossians 3:5-11:

> 5 Put to death therefore what is earthly in you: sexual immorality, impurity, passion, evil desire, and covetousness, which is idolatry. 6 On account of these the wrath of God is coming. 7 In these you too once walked, when you were living in them. 8 But now you must put them all away: anger, wrath, malice, slander, and obscene talk from your mouth.9 Do not lie to one another, seeing that you have put off the old self with its practices 10 and have put on the new self, which is being renewed in knowledge after the image of its creator. 11 Here there is not Greek and Jew, circumcised and uncircumcised, barbarian, Scythian, slave, free; but Christ is all, and in all.

Pruning to Prevent Pride

The second type of pruning is to minimize the height of the tree keeping it from growing too tall. If a tree is too tall, it may inhibit the farmer's ability to harvest his crops easily, resulting in spoiled fruit.

When we begin to grow and mature rapidly in God, it is in our nature to become prideful and entitled, especially if others start seeing our potential to produce mighty crops. When a tall tree produces fruit, it is difficult for the farmer to reach the fruits that are high in the branches. Those ones rot in the tree. Growing up in the Caribbean, I have seen this happen many times.

The home where I grew up had three huge mango trees. As children, my siblings and I would wait patiently for the mangoes to fall. Sometimes we were impatient and would get a bamboo stick to beat the fruit off the trees. Numerous times, we would race for a mango that fell only to see it was rotten or the birds had gotten to it before it fell from the tree. The fruit of pride is rotten and often manifests in ways such as:

1. Thinking more highly of ourselves than we should
2. Becoming ungrateful
3. Having a know-it-all attitude
4. Insensitive to the feelings of others
5. Resenting correction
6. Not submissive
7. Lacking respect
8. Thinking you are humble when you really are not

The fruit of pride can also show up as being fearful, people pleasing or even in our inability to make decisions. God has shown me all these traits in my life. At first, I couldn't believe it. The Holy Spirit had to show me each of these things in myself, and He used people to do it.

The Word of God describes a number of characteristics we should display as God's children

- Humility (Matthew 23:12)
- Gratitude (Colossians 1:12)
- Being submissive to each other (1 Corinthians 1:10). We must not seek to please others so much to be in their good graces that we stop listening to God (Galatians 1:10)
- We are to be sensitive to the needs of others (Romans 15:2).

When our growth leads to pride be prepared for pruning from the hands of God. In my last book *Caged: Your Scars, His Purpose,* I spoke about killing the pride in our lives.

It is very easy to become prideful, but hard to recognize the pride in our lives. It takes on many disguises. Hence, it becomes even more difficult for us to let God kill it. When we see the pride in our lives, we hide behind shame, but the funny thing is shame is also a manifestation of pride. Pride is so cunning it will only expose certain qualities of itself, not others.

> Everyone who is arrogant in heart is an abomination to the LORD; be assured, he will not go unpunished (Proverbs 16:5). –

Pride is a strong man. Once he takes hold of your life, he doesn't let go very easily. If pride is not crucified and buried in us, we are in for a great fall. It will be so mighty that others around us will be able to see it. Pride caused Lucifer to fall from the heavenly realm. It is one of Satan's greatest holds on the lives of human beings. We know the Word of God says in the book of Proverbs, "Pride goes before destruction." If you recognize any of the symptoms of pride in you, I urge you to humble yourself before God has to humble you.

God wants to produce fruit in your life, but the fruit we bear must be good. If all we produce is bad fruit, we will leave a nasty taste in the lives of others. We will give them stomachaches if they happen to eat from the rotten fruit we are producing.

So, you see, pruning is not only beneficial to our lives, but it is also essential to the lives of others we encounter daily, as well as the ones we are yet to encounter.

We look at the lives of many public figures and see the fruit of pride on display. This is because they didn't allow their characters to be refined by pruning before the light of their platform was shed on them.

Aggressive Pruning to Remove the Branches

The third and final basic type of pruning is an aggressive pruning where the farmer removes all the branches except for the main ones. This type of pruning is so drastic it may feel as if we are never going to recover. Our lives are basically stripped of everything we hold dear and precious to us. The only thing that remains is our foundation in Christ, which keeps us grounded and confident of our place in God despite the loss of things and people.

The dead things and people in our lives that no longer serve a purpose must be removed for us to continue to be full of life and vigor. We tend to hold on to things so dearly that when God wants to remove them from us, the pain we experience is excruciating. If we would just surrender control of our wills and trust that God knows what He is doing – because He does – then the level of pain we experience will not be so harsh. Pain during the pruning season is a guarantee. But how much pain we experience depends on the level of resistance we put up.

It's so funny now; looking back, the people I thought I couldn't live without are just memories. The things I thought I needed, I found out were not really needs but wants. God promised to supply all our needs (Philippians 4:19). It has been proven time and time again the heart only seeks the things that will bring it satisfaction in this life but are useless in the world to come. Our hearts' desires should always be heaven centered first. Afterward, all the things on the earth that are essential, God will graciously supply.

Christians often say to each other: "You are so heavenly-minded that you are no earthly good." In other words, the believer is so focused on the things of God, he or she does not entertain the things in this life. Though I understand the concept behind this quote, I still tend to disagree with it. Yes! We are to occupy until Christ returns; we are to live in freedom. However, Christians of today have taken this too far. Actually, we are so earthly focused that we are no heavenly good. How can we be the catalyst for change in this world if the world is not distinguishable from us? Therefore, a harsh pruning is done not only on individuals but on the ecclesia. God is cutting away the things that the church as the body and bride of Christ has been indulging in for far too long.

Each type of pruning has its place and level of importance in the life of a tree. The farmer decides which type of pruning he will perform. One important thing to know about the pruning process is that trees are mostly pruned during the resting stage. This is the point when the tree has stopped growing. Why is it important to wait for this stage to prune? To prevent the tree from looking scarred when it does begin to grow again.

The wounds the tree receives during the resting period will disappear when the tree begins to grow again. When we are lukewarm and God starts His breaking process, it is for our good. On the other side, our scars will not be that visible. We will have testimonies to encourage someone else on this journey.

It is amazing that Christ compares the believer to trees, and He prunes us at the right time and in the right season. On this Christian journey, we walk through these different types of pruning when many things are clogging up our hearts and decaying our thought life. At these times, God thins out our branches, so that we may receive the valued nutrients and oxygen we need to flourish. He removes the love of the world and the pleasures of life from our thoughts. The lifestyles of the world and the things in the world are huge distractions to believers. They are hindrances to the growth and production God wants to be evident in our lives.

Action Step: search your heart for any and all indications of pride in your life. We may tell ourselves that there is no pride in our hearts, but one thing I have learned in my seasons of being pruned is that pride likes to mask itself. In this case, we must ask God to expose it. Do not be alarmed if you find pride in your insecurities, doubts or even in fear. Once pride is exposed, the only thing left to do is surrender and submit to God in humility. Then watch God rid you of pride.

Chapter 10

The Secret of Brokenness

> But grow in the grace and knowledge of our Lord and Savior Jesus Christ to Him be the glory, both now and to the day of eternity. Amen (2 Peter 3:18).

After the pruning, the first signs of fruit-bearing begin to show. This is the blossoming stage as we truly take on the character of Christ. Our speech has changed from filthy to wholesome. Where we once walked in pride, humility can now be seen in us. The peace of God begins to manifest in our thinking and interactions with others. People can physically see a change in us. Some call it a glow, but it is the glory of God. Our prayer lives are on point as we continually tell others about the love of the Father, as well as His mercy and goodness towards them. The character of a Christian is very important in drawing others to the Father.

Our Christian character is the beginning stage of the fruit of the Spirit, which is love, joy, peace, patience, kindness, goodness, faithfulness, gentleness, and self-control (Galatians 5:22-23). The fruit of the Spirit is only developed as a result of the pruning done to our Christian character. However, after the development of the fruit comes the hardest part. We must now endure the crushing. The fruit of the Spirit must be crushed or tested to produce the anointing of God.

The anointing of God is matured love also called *agape* love. Many Christians walk around believing they cannot love another person unconditionally because they have not gone through the crushing, which activates the power to walk in unconditional love. The God-kind of love in us longs to be matured and perfected. It is only this mature and perfect love that can cast out all fear.

For the duration of this book, we will focus on love and the crushing we must endure to produce the anointing of God, which is love. Everything we must do on this earth for God has to be done through and in love. Love is the secret weapon that will bring this world to its knees. Love is the end product of brokenness. If love is left out of the equation, then all our efforts are just "works" or performances only to be seen and applauded by men. Our labors of love will always produce fragrances that are irresistible to the world. It's like a magnet that draws others to individuals walking in this type of love.

The anointing of love is the secret of brokenness. Love is the reason God takes His time to prune us during our developing stages. Love is the reason God crushes us, not once, but numerous times. Just like there are different stages to the pruning process, there are also different types of crushing. Varying levels of oil are produced for multiple purposes. No believer is exempt from this phase of life. The maturity of love in us depends on us dying to ourselves and submitting to the crushing of the fruit that our lives will produce. Scripture gives us various examples of biblical characters who went through the crushing process.

One thing to note about the crushing in the Bible is that it almost always took place in isolation away from the eyes of loved ones. We have examples of Moses being in the desert; that was his crushing phase away from his people. Joseph's crushing phase was his enslavement in Egypt, especially his time in prison isolated from his father and brothers. Jonah's crushing was in the belly of a fish, isolated because of his disobedience. David's crushing was running from Saul even though he was the future king of Israel. Our greatest example of crushing was our Lord as He journeyed from the garden of Gethsemane all the way to the cross.

God was with these individuals during their greatest moments of despair and pain; He will also be with us, even though our emotions will tell us differently. Emotions are some of the biggest deceivers in our lives apart from the Enemy himself. They will cause us to see and hear things that are not the truth. Emotions push us out of position because of opposition. We must win the fight of giving up by conquering our emotions.

Our lives as Christians will undergo continuous crushing whilst we are in this world until our Lord appears in the clouds of glory. Just like pruning is essential to the character development of the saints, the crushing is also necessary. Otherwise, we will never fully walk in our kingdom assignment as representatives of heaven. For us to represent heaven correctly God uses pruning and crushing to make us into His masterpieces on display.

We must be willing to submit to the pruning and crushing process. The world needs us to do so. They are desperately trying to escape their condition and the cage they are confined to because of their cruel master Satan. They are losing hope, which is evident in their current actions and lifestyles. We must not be fooled by their partying and apparent pleasures. Those looks of enjoyment should not be taken at face value. Most of the time, they are just facades. The veil of darkness we have all experienced before coming to Christ has a way of altering our perception. We believe things are just fine.

> The people living in darkness have seen a great light; on those living in the land of the shadow of death a light has dawned (Matthew 4:16).

It is only when the light of love penetrates the darkness that they can truly see their conditions. The Word says, "How can they hear without a preacher." Our lives are living epistles, and we are ministers of the gospel charged with carrying the light of love to the Enemy's camp. We must become willing vessels filled with the anointing to rescue the souls of men. The Holy Spirit will convict men when we completely surrender our wills to Him and demonstrate we have done so by our lifestyles.

Chapter 11

It Takes Pressure

3 You know that under pressure, your faith-life is forced into the open and shows its true colors. 4 So don't try to get out of anything prematurely. Let it do its work so you become mature and well-developed, not deficient in any way (James 1: 3-4).

Christians are like olives. It takes a lot of pressure to release the oil from us. The crushing and pressing of olives release the oil on the inside, which is then used in various ways. We are olives, and our lives must be crushed to release the content on the inside.

The weight of the crushing causes us to cry out in pain, anger, frustration, and utter hopelessness. It is so intense, the furthest thing from our minds and hearts during the crushing process is love. How could God allow us to go through so much pain yet expect us to serve Him? This is a question we are likely to ask when we are being crushed. The inner battle between what our spirits know and understand and what our souls and flesh refuse to see is the cause of the pain we experience during the process.

The olive goes through many different levels to release its oil. Our lives mirror the olive as we go through different stages of releasing the anointing on our lives. Olives are not allowed to ripen on the tree as most fruits are. Instead, when it's time to harvest, the farmer takes a long stick and he beats the fruit off the tree. Any remaining fruit will be physically shaken off the branches thereby freeing the tree of its fruit.

Our Savior went through this beating process for our sake. He endured the pain to redeem us unto Himself, and we are no greater than our Savior. In His Word, He lets us know there will be tribulation and trials in this life but to take courage because He has already overcome the world. Christ said we will be pressed and beaten down by life as He was, but we must endure to the end.

We cannot see the oil that is released every time we are crushed or the strength and wisdom that is produced when we endure the trials of life. His oil is only seen in our interaction with others who are going through the pressing stage we just left. This oil gives us the grace to meet and encourage others where they are on this faith journey. This oil is the anointing of God called love. The anointing of love is the product of the fruit of love.

In days gone by, before the invention of machinery to do the processing, olives were placed on a grinder's wheel. This was the initial step in the process. A big stone wheel turned by oxen or donkeys crushed the fruit to a pulp. Tiny drops of oil were released into a receiving container. The olive was then pressed until nothing was left to come forth. To get everything out of the olive, it would take about four different pressings. Each press produced a different type of oil for separate purposes. The first oil pressed is normally the purest oil known as extra virgin olive oil. Then there is the virgin oil. The third and fourth are pressed oil.

In the ancient days, the first pressed oil was used for lighting the lamps, the second for anointing, the third for cleansing by making soap and the fourth and least common for cooking.

As Christians, the first thing that comes out of us when we are crushed and pressed is the light of Christ. This light becomes a beacon for the entire world to see. Then the anointing comes to enable us to do the works of Christ. It's the anointing on our lives that will break yokes and chains off the lives of others. The third pressing is the oil that will bring healing. It's a grace of compassion to cover a multitude of sins. This world needs healing and cleansing. The love of Jesus cleanses us from all sin. When this love is activated in the lives of believers, we can forgive others. In turn, it brings healing to their hurting hearts.

Lastly, the oil used for cooking represents a new and revived sense of fellowship with other believers when we complete our process. It also means we will not turn a blind eye to the physical needs of the destitute and poor.

The oil used for cooking is just as important as the first oil. We must be the type of people who will use all of the oil God produces in us. We cannot want the first three anointings but not the last oil produced. The last oil produced is the one that will get our hands dirty.

In the natural when we prepare food, handling the ingredients may cause us to get dirty; some may get on our clothing. Our hands may become dirty. To be fully used by God, we must serve the saints and the sinners alike. We must be prepared to get dirty and also to serve others without receiving so much as a thank you. We must be ready to listen to the critics speak about the things we are doing to help others. Moreover, we must be prepared to feed others without expectations.

The benefits of the crushing will never be experienced if we run away from the pain of it all. For me, the crushing did seem harsh and unfair but on the other side of the pain, I found freedom and joy. The struggle takes place in your minds. One day, the mind is determined to make it to the end but the next, the thoughts are tormenting, to say the least. They are tormenting in the sense that the Enemy will relentlessly taunt you to abort the process. He will make you question your identity as a child of God. For this reason, God allows our foundation in Him to be solidified before the crushing.

Olives are bitter to the taste. The only way to rid them of this bitterness is to crush them. It's very interesting to see folks who were once very bitter and angry transformed by God. After going through a hard time and then encountering Christ, they become loving and kind.

Just as the olives need to be crushed to get rid of bitterness so must all believers when we come to Christ. We lived so long in sin that our sinful nature is very strong-willed and prideful. We are very rough around the edges and possess filthy attitudes. We carry the stench of sin and the behaviors of the kingdom of darkness. Sanctification is necessary. This is the process whereby Christ changes us into His likeness. While sanctification is a process, it needs our voluntary participation to transform us into the image of Christ. Failure to submit will cause the sanctification process to seem extremely difficult and lengthy.

Defying the changes God wants to make in our lives opens the doorway for the Enemy to whisper lies in our ears and deceive us. If we are not careful, we will find ourselves in a backslidden condition wondering how we got there. Don't fight the cleansing and the pressing. As hard as it is for me to say this, I will: if God allows me to go through pain, it says I am worth it. He loves me too much to let me stay the same.

Love is very mysterious at times. It involves emotions because of our inability to accurately describe it and put it into words, but love is not an emotion as the dictionary defines it. Love is the genetic makeup of God that no scientist can ever study or get to the origin of.

I am grateful love cannot be defined and put into a neat little box. Otherwise, we would be able to do the same with God. No matter how hard human beings try to figure out God or define Him, they just can't do it. He is the best thing that happened to me. Knowing He loves me, an invisible speck in this vast universe is both overwhelming and scary. It's overwhelming because His presence leaves me speechless at times. It's also scary because the more I seek Him, the more I understand I shouldn't be welcome in His presence because of my sin nature. Grace then floods my heart and soul; the tears fall as I sit in utter reference to the King who calls me even closer. Love beckons, and grace covers.

When we come out on the other side of the crushing, the anointing of love will display some unusual qualities. These qualities will be discussed in their own chapters, but I have listed them here for you. When we allow our lives to be crushed, the mature and perfect agape love will put the following traits on display:

- The truth of love
- The servanthood of love
- The power of love
- The contagiousness of love
- The light of love
- The fellowship of love

There are many more qualities of the agape love of God at work in our lives. The agape love of God with its special anointing for human beings can't be contained within the pages of this book. There is still so much about the love of God that I will never understand until I see the Father one day. Until then I am content with writing what He has placed on my heart.

Chapter 12

The Truth of Love

> But speaking the truth in love, we are to grow up in all aspects into Him who is the head, even Christ (Ephesians 4:15).
>
> So, have I become your enemy by telling you the truth? (Galatians 4:16).

Usually, love is associated with softness, serenity, warm fuzzy feelings and comfort. However, there is a side to love we often neglect to talk about or even acknowledge: the in-your-face truth of love. One of the hardest things I had to hear was that I was still letting fear hold me hostage. Being told that cut me to the core. I didn't even know how to respond.

What does fear have to do with the truth of love? Everything! The Bible says perfect love casts out all fear. When we are fully engaged and filled with the love of God fear won't be a factor in our lives. Fear says don't trust God because He is not a man of His word. Fear says God doesn't have the best for you, and you are wasting your time serving a God who watches you suffer. Fear says to turn your back on God and figure out your life on your own. Fear says don't surrender everything to God because there is no point in giving Him your all. Fear says a lot of things that are not the truth according to the Word of God. Yet, we continually play hide-and-seek with God using our hearts.

One moment we are all in, and the next minute, we are living in total chaos because we chose to listen to the lies of the Enemy. This back and forth is to be expected during the crushing because we cannot see what is coming out of us due to the darkness and the pain we are experiencing. It is said that fear is false evidence appearing real, but I would say fear can sometimes be **real evidence allowed to reign.** Fear is sent to hold you hostage. It is meant to prevent you from moving forward and conquering territories still unclaimed.

> For God has not given us a spirit of fear, but of power and of love and of a sound mind (2 Timothy 1:7).

Everything in us wants to control the outcome of our lives but this life cannot be controlled using human will. It is only by yielding our lives to an unchanging God that we will find true freedom. Freedom is found in the truth that God loves us unconditionally.

It may seem unfair when your life is at a standstill, while everyone around you is moving along. This is when the truth of God's words must be applied. It is also the time when you must search your soul and find the reason you are standing still. The majority of the time, you will discover the reason you are not moving forward is because of fear, as well as your inability to let go and be led blindly by God.

When the first sign of the anointing of love starts flowing, we will realize love is the face of truth. We will hear some very harsh truths about ourselves, and we must be OK with it, knowing that it's for our benefit. Do not be offended by the person revealing the truth to you. Most of us don't like to hear the truth about ourselves. We would rather live in denial than to admit we are far from perfect. We want to maintain a certain image in the eyes of others; hence, we constantly miss the cues God is sending to push us further in life.

The crushing reveals our weaknesses and faulty thinking. We cannot talk about what love is and the many adventures love has for us as the people of God if we cannot deal with our inner demons. We tend to see our insecurities in others.

One of the reasons people are so critical today is because of the mirror effect. The mirror image of ourselves is often seen in the lives of people we meet on a regular basis. We tend to see our flaws in the lives of others. It irritates us because we cannot fix people, so we critique their lives. The truth is we cannot even fix ourselves; we need God to do that for us. Look at what it says in the book of Romans about judging. A judging spirit is a critical spirit:

> Therefore, you have no excuse, O man, every one of you who judges. For in passing judgment on another you condemn yourself, because you, the judge, practice the very same things. We know that the judgment of God rightly falls on those who practice such things. Do you suppose, O man—you who judge those who practice such things and yet do them yourself—that you will escape the judgment of God? (Romans 2:1-3 ESV).

Love is unbreakable, and it can handle anything that is thrown at it. When I speak about love, I am not talking about the human definition of love. No! I am talking about the agape love of God that chases us down to have a relationship with us. I am talking about the God-kind of love that is so obsessed with you and me it will tell us the things we don't want to hear. This kind of love pushes aside our defenses. It erases the accumulated evidence life has on us without ever reminding us of our filthy past. This love is indescribable.

Life has taught many of us to snuggle up with fear because it will keep us safe. But is fear really keeping us safe or is it keeping us from seeing all life has to offer? It is so easy to slip back into a cage mentality. Unknowingly, I was slowing rebuilding a cage because I became at ease in my comfort zone. Had it not been for a random Saturday afternoon phone call I would never have realized this truth.

The crushing of our lives produces the oil of love, but it also exposes and rids us of the hidden impurities. Familiarity is a companion of fear. When these two work together, we are often caught in an inescapable trap if God doesn't step in and save us.

Familiarity causes believers to easily fall into sin, while love hopes and believes that one day, we will come to our senses and fully embrace it. The spirit of familiarity is exposed during the crushing as an impure factor that will be discarded at the end of the process. If the anointing of love and the impurity (familiarity) are not separated during the crushing, our love will be contaminated. It will need to be purified before being used.

Chapter 13

Love Is a Servant

> And above all things have fervent charity among yourselves: for charity shall cover the multitude of sins. 9 Use hospitality one to another without grudging. 10 As every man hath received the gift, even so minister the same one to another, as good stewards of the manifold grace of God (1 Peter 4:8-10).

Falling in love by the world's standards often leads us into the trap of loving others with expectations. We expect if we love our families, friends, spouses, boyfriends, and girlfriends, they will return that same level of love to us. However, that is often not the case, especially when it comes to those closest to us. These are the very ones we experience the most hurt and pain from in life. This type of pain can lead to decades of confusion and inner turmoil.

As Christians, we are commanded to love unconditionally, which means loving regardless of the pain we may endure. How can we love unconditionally if we are not crushed to learn about empathy? Empathy allows us to feel compassion for others because we had similar experiences. The crushing takes us on a journey to bring out servanthood in us. The anointing of love activates true servanthood, and God remembers our labors of love as it says in Hebrews 6:10:

> 10 For God is not unrighteous to forget your work and labour of love, which ye have shewed toward his name, in that ye have ministered to the saints, and do minister.

It is tough to put aside the flesh and become a servant of others. A servant has no right to complain about how he is treated. I know this is not popular in today's society where everyone is demanding rights. However, when we look at the monarchical kingdoms, the servant is a subject of the king and queen. He or she has to do the king or queen's bidding regardless of how demoralizing it may be. Servants cannot argue with the king or refuse to obey; such actions may result in fines, imprisonment or worse – death. It is against the law to disobey the king in the natural. Yet, we, the subjects of the highest King are very bold in our disobedience to Him.

Why do believers who serve the King of kings often rebel against Him? Why do we resist the one we call the Lord of our lives, the one who is supposedly our sovereign Savior and Master? Luke 12:41-48 speaks about the unfaithful servant who disregarded his master's duty because he wasn't in sight. We are living our lives like this unfaithful servant because we are not urgent in doing our Father's will. In the natural, the king of the kingdom has all the power and authority. The natural world is a reflection of the spiritual world; therefore, as servants of God, we are out of order to rebel against Him.

The mercy and grace of our heavenly King is unorthodox. He does not deal with us according to our arrogance. He left His throne in heaven to become a servant. He is our example of how to govern our lives here on the earth. We are citizens of heaven and ambassadors to the earth. But many of us are abandoning our posts to mingle with the kingdom of darkness.

> Be ye therefore followers of God, as dear children; 2 And walk in love, as Christ also hath loved us, and hath given himself for us

> an offering and a sacrifice to God for a sweet smelling savour (Ephesians 5:1-2).

An ambassador in the natural has diplomatic immunity in any country he is stationed. This means he is not subjected to punishment from the country in which he is an ambassador. We have immunity from the Enemy of this world but we are abandoning our posts to mingle with the darkness. As such, we are left defenseless. In the natural, if an ambassador abandons his post, he is seen as a traitor to his home country. Severe consequences will follow. Every time we choose our flesh over the spirit, we are siding with the Enemy, the traitor of heaven and the tormentor of the earth.

> It is for freedom that Christ has set us free. Stand firm, then, and do not let yourselves be burdened again by a yoke of slavery (Galatians 5:1).

As servants and ambassadors of Christ, please don't give into the system of the world and its definition of love. Search the law book of heaven, and read all about what our King says about love.

Those who demonstrate the love modeled by heaven will always reflect the hearts of servants and walk in humility. 1

Corinthians Chapter 13 is a blueprint for how love is demonstrated from the heart of a humble servant. Jesus the servant-King totally turned the world upside down with His method of showing love. His humble beginnings on earth (being born in a stable) showed us love will take the lowest form and grab our attention. The stable where the animals slept is a depiction of where the lowest amongst us live. They have nothing to offer but themselves.

The stable marked the beginning of a journey that would eventually lead to death on a cross, the ultimate price of love. The love of God is indescribable and unattainable through works. In other words, we cannot work for the love of God. Nothing we do will ever measure up to the price of His love. The world cannot understand the love of God, so they question it. They weigh it against the world's standards of love based on our emotional makeup. The love of God is only received by faith in the Son of God when we walk in the Spirit and not the flesh, but this love must grow, mature, and reproduce. The flesh is where our emotions live, and the flesh cannot please God.

Because the love of God is spiritual it must be received spiritually. However, we can still experience the tangible presence of the love of God. The love of God has the anointing to do damage to the kingdom of darkness. This anointing can only come from a crushing. As newborn babes we receive the agape love. However, we fail to realize this love is only a seed, which must develop and grow within us. The Word of God says we grow from faith to faith. It is the same thing for the love of God. It's to be matured and perfected in us.

> But whoso keepeth his word, in him verily is the love of God perfected: hereby know we that we are in him (1 John 2:5).

When this love has been perfected then and only then will we be free of the fear that brings judgment.

> Forasmuch then as Christ hath suffered for us in the flesh, arm yourselves likewise with the same mind: for he that hath suffered in the flesh hath ceased from sin (1 Peter 4:1).

The anointing that comes from the crushing is the agape love, which has been perfected. It is also the supernatural power that will allow us to do the greater works Christ said we will do.

> Verily, verily, I say unto you, He that believeth on me, the works that I do shall he do also; and greater works than these shall he do; because I go unto my Father (John 14:12).

Love takes the place of a servant so the world can take notice and turn to the Father. It is vital that Christians have the hearts of servants as witnesses to the world.

> Have this mind among yourselves, which is yours in Christ Jesus, who, though he was in the form of God, did not count equality with God a thing to be grasped, but made himself nothing, taking the form of a servant, being born in the likeness of men. And being found in human form, he humbled himself by becoming obedient to the point of death, even death on a cross (Philippians 2:5-8 ESV).

Chapter 14
Love Is Bold

> Seeing ye have purified your souls in obeying the truth through the Spirit unto unfeigned love of the brethren, see that ye love one another with a pure heart fervently (1 Peter 1:22).

I have no clue how to explain the love of God because it far surpasses all my earthly knowledge and everything I have encountered here on the earth. It overwhelms my heart and soul whenever I think of me and the person I know myself to be. The love of God causes my heart to respond in praise and worship. Gratitude captivates my every thought.

> It is of the LORD'S mercies that we are not consumed, because his compassions fail not (Lamentations 3:22 KJV).

John Newton penned these lyrics of the famous song "Amazing Grace":

> Amazing grace how sweet the sound
> That saved a wretch like me
> I once was lost but now I am found
> Was blind but now I see

This song gives us a small glimpse of the love of God. Today, the song that captivates my heart is the "Reckless Love of God." The words "reckless" and "God" just don't seem to belong together. We picture God as a gentleman who never imposes His will on our ability to think, reason, and make choices.

The word "reckless" is usually associated with someone who doesn't care, someone very bossy and pushy, someone who is not careful. Yet, this is a side of God people the world over need to encounter. Just as the song says, there is nothing God won't do to bring us to Him, so we can experience His love and joy. It's the reason He allowed His Son to die a sinner's death when He never even sinned. He lived a perfect sinless life, and God allowed Him to take the place of sinful man.

God's love is unsearchable; it is immeasurable and unexplainable. This fact about God keeps mankind at arm's length. We want to figure out God and be able to explain the simple things we as human beings ask each other. For example, who created God? Where did He come from? These questions have plagued the minds of humans for centuries. Anything mankind cannot explain, we often want to explain away.

At times, I keep Him at arm's length because His love for me just doesn't make sense. Everything in me does not want to trust this love. Humanly speaking, past failures say God shouldn't love me. Fleshly speaking, love has always been a step away from my reach. You will never be able to chase and catch something you already have because you're not self-aware. Take a dog, for example, he sees and feels his tail twitching; yet, somehow, he concludes he must catch that twitching tail. He proceeds to chase the very thing he already has in his possession.

At times, we chase after love in all the wrong things, places, people, and situations. After our pursuits, we are left feeling unwanted and not good enough; hopelessness and despair take over our lives. Imagine the people in the world who don't know God. They live with a sense of dread every day believing God wants nothing to do with them. Think about the countless people who are searching for love, but they don't understand what they are really searching for is God Himself who is love.

How many times have you looked at a dog chasing his tail around in circles and laughed at his stupidity? We fail to realize we look as foolish as the dog; the only difference is we are chasing love, while he is pursuing his tail. We are even bigger dummies because we are the superior beings, the top of the food chain so to speak.

We are yet to see the love of God is crazy and relentless when it comes to us human beings. The angels can't figure it out. The Enemy is mad and still scratching his head trying to come to terms with God's love for us. The fact that God gives us numerous second chances but he didn't get any makes Satan mad. He got thrown out of heaven the moment he tried to overthrow God.

The love of God releases us to live boldly. The perfect love of God casts out all fear. That's the life I am pursuing. I want to be so perfected in the love of God that all fear will be gone. We can honestly admit that while we are brave in some areas, some things still scare the crap out of us. What would it look like if we had no fear on the earth? We would be free to do exploits for the kingdom of God. But better still, we would create a ripple effect on the earth causing people to accept and surrender to the reckless love of God. As we demonstrate God's love to those around us, they will take notice. Loving each other and living in community will open the eyes of the world to the love of God.

Boldness is often seen in the lives of the great men and women of the Bible after they experienced bouts of uncertainty and timidity. The love of God produces boldness. God sees exactly where we are currently when it comes to manifesting the perfect love of God. It's OK to not fully understand the love of God. However, it's time to place all of our uncertainties and doubts into the hands of love. Love - matured love - is desperately fighting to be put on display in our lives.

The world needs to see the body of Christ is just that, the body. It's time to stop chasing our tails, stand still for a moment, and grab hold of what we already possess. The moment a dog stands still, he can put his tail in his mouth. And so it is with us as well; the moment we quiet ourselves and sit in stillness, is the moment we sense the presence of God, which is the manifestation of His love. Everything about God is done in love. As a judge, when He weighs our actions on His scale, it's from His heart of righteous love that He decides our fate.

Love so bold to correct will seal our sentences whether we chose to serve Him or not. It breaks God's heart to see many on the way to a Christless eternity. He is equally hurt to see believers who have experienced and know His love selfishly hoard it by keeping it to ourselves. When we surrender to God we love and live boldly through the power of God living inside us. We must rely on the Holy Spirit to lead and teach us about expressing bold love.

Our unwillingness to fully surrender to the Holy Spirit's leading and gentle whispers keeps us living in fear and blocks our ability to walk boldly in love. Bold love brings a drastic transformation to our lives that will go where our very lives are in danger, and the threat won't even make us second guess. As in the life of Paul, bold love was put on display multiple times. He was very content and unshaken in his faith. Bold love is unshakable faith even while looking death straight in the eye.

Every Bible character that did exploits for God possessed this bold love. Some may have feared and questioned God in the beginning, but in the end, their love, or rather, their trust in God set them on a path of radical obedience. When we surrender our all to Jesus and give Him full control, we are saying, "God, I trust You. Even though my eyes and my mind may be uncertain because of the circumstances I am presently seeing, I choose to believe you. Surrender and trust are very necessary for bold love to be activated.

Prayer: God I want to be perfected in the love that casts out all fear. I am courageous sometimes, but at other times, I struggle to trust You and be bold. However, I want to live a life that is completely filled with Your perfect love. Highlight every part of me that doubts Your love, and I will surrender it to You. You are a good Father, and Your desire is to put Your love on display in my life for the world to see You and know the great love You have for them. Jesus, thank You for the sacrifice of dying for my sins. I open my heart for You to dethrone what hinders my walk with You. I am Yours, Lord, now and forever. Amen.

Chapter 15
Contagious Love

> A new commandment I give to you, that you love one another: just as I have loved you, you also are to love one another. By this all people will know that you are my disciples, if you have love for one another (John 13:34-35 ESV).

The story of David brings out the love between David and Jonathan but not much is really said about David's love for Saul.

> And David came to Saul and stood before him: and he loved him greatly; and he became his armourbearer (1 Samuel 16:21).

We see David's love for Saul when David got news of his death and he mourns for both Saul and his best friend (2

Samuel 1:1-10). Mourning for Jonathan is understandable but for Saul? Yet, the Bible tells us that David wept and tore his clothing at the news of their death.

> 11 Then David took hold on his clothes, and rent them; and likewise, all the men that were with him:
>
> 12 And they mourned, and wept, and fasted until even, for Saul, and for Jonathan his son, and for the people of the LORD, and for the house of Israel; because they were fallen by the sword (2 Samuel 1:11-12).

He mourned so much that he composed a song for Saul and Jonathan and made all of Israel learn it. David went so far as to call Saul lovely. If you are not familiar with this story, I urge you to read it in the books of 1&2 Samuel. Saul was the reason David's wife Michal sneaked him out of the palace to save his life. Saul tried to kill David while he played music to calm the tormenting spirit that came upon Saul. Yet, David chose the word "lovely" to describe his enemy. The story of David, Saul, and Jonathan shows the depth of love. Love is so deep, it will overlook the faults of others. The love of God expects nothing in return from others. But we fail in love because we expect others to reciprocate our love.

Would you call someone lovely who tried to kill you numerous times? Would you describe someone who unjustly caused you to live in exile like a criminal lovely? Would you pass over the opportunity to get even with someone who is clearly out to get you? Would you make it your business to avenge the death of an enemy? Would you write a song about your enemy proclaiming his or her greatness and goodness?

The love of God was evident in David's life, whether he was protecting his sheep or followers. He fed the tired and weak. He avenged the death of a known enemy. He covered the faults of his enemy. Love gives your enemies a different perspective of you and lets them see the error of their ways like it did Saul:

> 16 When David had finished speaking these words to Saul, Saul said, "Is this your voice, my son David?" Then Saul lifted up his voice and wept. 17He said to David, "You are more righteous than I; for you have dealt well with me, while I have dealt wickedly with you (1 Samuel 24:16-17).

In Matthew 5:44, Jesus implores us to love our enemies. How are you treating your enemies? Do not forget to do good unto all men including the ones who are against you? Loving our enemies is not an easy task, but Jesus commands it; therefore, we must obey.

> But I say unto you, love your enemies, bless them that curse you, do good to them that hate you, and pray for them which despitefully use you, and persecute you (Matthew 5:44).

Peter tells us love does not expose the faults of others, but it conceals multitudes of sin. When we cover the sins of others, we demonstrate deep love.

> Most important of all, continue to show deep love for each other, for love covers a multitude of sins (1 Peter 4:8 NLT).

The night Jesus was betrayed, he gave a new commandment to the disciples. He told them that by their actions everyone will know they are His disciples. Jesus knew what Judas and Peter would have done long before they did it. Yet, He loved them and covered their sins. Jesus concealed the sins of both Peter and Judas when He washed His disciples' feet. Our feet carry the gospel of peace; it also means we must walk in peace continually. We cannot walk in peace if we don't continuously wash the dirt off our feet. We cannot carry a muddied gospel of peace to the world. At the end of each day, we must wash our minds and hands free of the contaminants of life's trials.

God requires us to walk in love. This love is called agape; it is contagious. Once you encounter this kind of love, you become infected. Consequently, everyone you come into contact with also becomes infected with this love. The early church had a contagious love for God, and they extended it to the lost, hurting, broken, and dying world, as well as to each other in the body of Christ.

> 9 But as touching brotherly love ye need not that I write unto you: for ye yourselves are taught of God to love one another.
> 10 And indeed ye do it toward all the brethren which are in all Macedonia: but we beseech you, brethren, that ye increase more and more (1 Thessalonians 4:9-10).

This kind of love is hard to put into words but once you experience it, there is no denying. It cannot be contained; you can't control it. You just can't kill it. Many have tried and failed, and many are still trying, but they too shall fail. God is love. He can't be killed. The love of God forms a community. It grows rapidly when allowed to flourish. It breaks down barriers, and you can't fight against it. When we gave our hearts to Christ, we received this agape love. In the same way our faith in Christ must grow and mature, the agape love inside of us must also grow and mature beyond its initial birth at salvation. If we let the love of God grow and bloom, it will break down the barriers in our lives and the lives of others.

> For Christ himself has brought peace to us. He united Jews and Gentiles into one people when, in his own body on the cross, he broke down the wall of hostility that separated us (Ephesians 2:14 NLT).

When love begins to mature in our lives, it rids us of any and all excuses to remain the same. If we are fighting to remain the same, it means we are suffocating the love of God in us. We will not mature if we continue doing this.

And as we live in God, our love grows more perfect. So, we will not be afraid on the day of judgment, but we can face him with confidence because we live like Jesus here in this world (1 John 4:17 NLT).

Love turns the prideful person into a humble person. It rids us of our jealous tendencies, kills the gossiping spirit, covetousness, the judgmental spirit, and self. And when self-dies, our eyes are finally open to see our neighbors, as God sees them because we see ourselves in our neighbors.

When we see our neighbors through Christ's eyes, our hearts will break, and we will weep and mourn for our enemies. We will weep for our brothers and sisters in our local churches. We will weep for those around the world who are dying daily for their faith and belief in a God who gives contagious love. We will weep for our communities, state, nation and for the world. We will not only see the hurt, brokenness, desperation, and the cries of this world, but we will feel the pain they experience daily on their way to a Christless eternity with no hope.

1With Christ as my witness, I speak with utter truthfulness. My conscience and the Holy

Spirit confirm it. **2** My heart is filled with bitter sorrow and unending grief **3** for my people, my Jewish brothers and sisters. I would be willing to be forever cursed—cut off from Christ! —if that would save them (Romans 9:1-3).

We will weep because we realize we have been selfish in the way we treat each other, even those we worship with on a weekly basis. Some of the things we do that are not pleasing to God are:

- Looking down on each other
- Failing to acknowledge each other's presence in a room or on the street
- Showing favoritism
- A general lack of genuine concern for each other

We could add to this list if we are brave and honest enough to face the ugly truth about ourselves. James 4:1-2 explains why we have so many conflicts:

What is causing the quarrels and fights among you? Don't they come from the evil desires at war within you? 2 You want what you don't have, so you scheme and kill to get it. You are jealous of what others have, but you can't get it, so you fight and wage war to take it away from them (James 4:1-2).

Our current spiritual condition can be measured by the way we love others. If our love for God is in a gray area, then we tend to treat others the same way. We show an "iffy" kind of love. Our love becomes conditional instead of unconditional. Yet, Christ commands us to love our neighbors as ourselves.

> [13] For you have been called to live in freedom, my brothers and sisters. But don't use your freedom to satisfy your sinful nature. Instead, use your freedom to serve one another in love. [14] For the whole law can be summed up in this one command: "Love your neighbor as yourself." [15] But if you are always biting and devouring one another, watch out! Beware of destroying one another.

> ¹⁶ So I say, let the Holy Spirit guide your lives. Then you won't be doing what your sinful nature craves (Galatians 5:13-16).

We need a love revolution inside of us, a reset to change our view of ourselves and each other. The world is depending on us. We must let brotherly love continue by allowing it to flow. We all fall short sometimes and conflicts will arise between us as a family, but it must not stop the flow of love. God's love is compassionate; it is unashamed; it is enthusiastic. It forces us to abandon our preconceived ideas about each other and just love without pretense despite our many faults.

> 9 Don't just pretend to love others. Really love them. Hate what is wrong. Hold tightly to what is good. 10 Love each other with genuine affection and take delight in honoring each other (Romans 12:9-10 NLT).
>
> Love never gives up, never loses faith, is always hopeful, and endures through every circumstance (1 Corinthians 13:7).

Love is intentional. We must give and receive love on purpose. Love says, "You hurt me, but I am purposely loving you anyway. We can't agree on anything. I am going to love you on purpose."

> 4Remain in me, as I also remain in you. No branch can bear fruit by itself; it must remain in the vine. Neither can you bear fruit unless you remain in me (John 15:4).

Loving each other as Christ loved us means sacrificing your comforts for another. It means giving up control of your will and the ability to control your life. To grow in this contagious, passionate, and intentional love of God, we must surrender all to Jesus. So, the key to loving our brothers and sisters in Christ is to surrender all the areas of our lives we don't want to lose control of. That way, Christ's love can flow freely and continually in and out. It will radically transform us for His glory and use us to help our fellow believers, as well as the world at large.

Chapter 16
The Light of Love

This is the message which we have heard from Him and declare to you, that God is light and in Him is no darkness at all (1 John 1:5 NKJV).

When Jesus walked on this earth, He did so in the spirit of truth. Truth is light; thus, when we walk in the truth, we are also walking in the light. When we fail to follow the teachings of Christ, we are no longer walking in the light but have shifted our walk toward the kingdom of darkness. Love always speaks the truth because love is a light.

This world needs the truth of the Word of God. However, Christians cannot tell the truth to the world if we are lying to each other. How do we lie to each other? Well, I am glad you asked. We lie to each other when we refuse to correct a brother or a sister who is going in the wrong direction. In doing so, we choose to walk in darkness by not highlighting the truth. Speaking the truth to each other is not the same as judging and condemning. Many times, when we speak to other believers about their lifestyles, we do it in a condemning manner. The Word of God teaches us a better way. It says we ought to restore each other in the spirit of love considering ourselves.

> Brethren, if a man be overtaken in a fault, ye which are spiritual, restore such an one in the spirit of meekness; considering thyself, lest thou also be tempted (Galatians 6:1 NKJV).

Speaking from experience, I would be the first to say that in the past, I was very harsh when I corrected others. I did so using the excuse that I was a straightforward individual who doesn't sugar coat anything. Nevertheless, with time, I realized I could speak the truth without compromise in a gentle loving manner. Using that method made people more receptive to what I had to say.

In Matthew 5:16, Jesus is explicit in His description of His followers. He said we are the light of the world and this light cannot be hid. When believers walk in love the light of Jesus shines brightly. On the other hand, when we fail to walk in love, the light of Christ grows dim within us. The love of

God that is within each of us must not be hidden. It should be a lighthouse guiding the unsaved to the safe harbor of salvation where they can receive Jesus as their Lord and Savior.

I am afraid that too many Christians are hiding their lights. They are too afraid to love people for fear of being hurt. Let's face it; the Word of God tells us that no servant is greater than his master. Jesus was mistreated for the love He showed to the destitute in His time. As our Master, we are to follow His lead. Therefore, He is calling us to put our feelings aside when we are hurt by others to demonstrate His love for the lost and downtrodden of our day.

Brokenness takes us to a place where we feel alone and unloved. It is like being in a dark pit where we come face-to-face with ourselves. We long for others to see the pain we are in and reach out a hand of comfort to us. There is nothing more painful than to see others pass you by with their noses turned up while you are suffering from life's trials. They fail to express the love of Christ.

Brokenness will change you from the inside out. On the other side of brokenness, you will not only recognize the pain of others, but you will also no longer stand idly by when they hurt. We will be quick to show compassion. Why? Because we will remember how it felt to be in that same position. It is easy to turn a blind eye and act superior when you have not felt the crushing pains of brokenness.

Loving others becomes easy when we see who they are inside; seeing demands action. If seeing is not followed by action, it means we have only made an observation. Do you see a need and turn a blind eye to it yet declare you are a loving person?

Brokenness sharpens our prayer life. When we are going through trials, we find time to pray – time we never had before. God knows exactly how much pressure to apply to us to bring us to a place of surrender. The light of love requires that we surrender to God and die to self, for it to be put on display brightly.

Too many times we hide our lights or we shine a blurred version of the light of Christ to the world. Brokenness is like a window cleaner that wipes the dirt off the lenses of our lamps, so it can burn brightly. Prayer is the cloth that is used to wipe the dirt when love is blurred.

Brokenness removes the covering that we use to cover the light of God on the inside of us. God deals with the issues in our lives that make us hide the light in the first place. Fear can cause us to hide our lights because we do not believe we have enough of the Word in us to share it with others. Our testimonies of how we came to Christ, along with the love of Christ in us are enough to draw the attention of the world. Even when we are trying to hide our lights, they peek out. God doesn't want our lives to be peep shows; He wants a full display. Brokenness is the route He allows us to travel on to put us on display.

Chapter 17

The Power of Love

So now faith, hope, and love abide, these three; but the greatest of these is love (1 Corinthians 13:13 ESV).

It takes a power greater than our will-power to love people who have hurt us deeply. In our strength, we do not possess the capacity to love others as Jesus told us to. God does not expect us to love others with the love of Jesus from our human emotions. Rather, He wants to make us mature in the love that comes only from Him. To love the way God loves will cost us something. The death of His Son is the price God paid for loving us.

I had the awesome experience of going through the pain of loving the people who used me for years as if it was nothing. I couldn't remain unforgiving. Every time my flesh tried to be mean and petty to those persons, God would give me a not so gentle nudge to remind me of His commandment to love. As much as I wanted to seek revenge, I couldn't, for the grace God showed me in my mess was ever before me speaking. When grace speaks, it is impossible to ignore her voice.

Imagine being there for a friend through all of her mess and then she tells you quite bluntly, "I am tired of you and your cycles!" The person no longer wants to be your friend. Without even a second thought, she moves on, while you are stuck in pain from the friendship that was lost.

Imagine still having to work with this person without showing any signs of unforgiveness or bitterness. Imagine having to lay aside your opinions and rights to give her a dose of her own medicine every time your paths crossed. This is where I learned to love as if I was never hurt. It was the most difficult thing to put into practice because a part of me was saying the opposite of what God commanded.

Your inner battle is a fight for the control of the throne of your heart. The flesh in me wanted to make that other person hurt like I was hurting. However, the spirit wanted me to grow up and see the situation from a different perspective. We cannot love if we don't forgive. Forgiveness is a prerequisite for loving others with the agape love of God. I wrestled with the thoughts of being mean and the command to forgive for months until I could love that person genuinely again. The more I wrestled with being petty, the more I felt the pain and the anguish of the loss. It is hard to love again after being wounded in your soul, but it can be done if you are willing to take self out of the picture.

During that time of wrestling internally with whether to obey God or do my own thing, there were days when I gave into the flesh and listened to my feelings about this person. But the Holy Spirit didn't allow those negative feelings to linger long. When I gave into the flesh with anger and bitterness the Holy Spirit brought conviction, and I was reminded of the grace of God. Grace will remind us of the love of God, and mercy will keep us from getting what we deserve.

Today, I can laugh and talk with this person as if I was never hurt by her. Are we friends? Not in the same sense we were before, but we have mutual respect for each other. Boundaries were put in place, and I have respect for the boundaries established, but I love her like a sibling you can't wish away. We may never be close again, but she is my sister in Christ; that makes her family. There is no sin in heaven, so we must learn how to live on the earth with our brethren whom we will see for eternity in heaven. Keep this scripture as a reminder when you are struggling to forgive and walk in love.

> 20 If a man say, I love God, and hateth his brother, he is a liar: for he that loveth not his brother whom he hath seen, how can he love God whom he hath not seen? 21And this commandment have we from him, That he who loveth God love his brother also (1 John 4:20).

When we live our lives thinking about eternity, we will walk like Peter said – circumspectly. We must decide whether we want to live outside the presence of God in hell or in the presence of God in heaven with the saints. Is it easy to love as God loves? No! The flesh has to be crucified daily by the power of the Holy Spirit within us to accomplish this. If left to our own way of thinking without the Spirit's leading, the flesh will always win and be in control. We must continually deny ourselves, as well as renew our minds daily. The scriptures below are important to know and also to memorize as you walk with Christ.

> And he said to [them] all, If any [man] will come after me, let him deny himself, and take up his cross daily, and follow me (Luke 9:23).
>
> I protest by your rejoicing which I have in Christ Jesus our Lord, I die daily (1 Corinthians 15:31).

> And be renewed in the spirit of your mind (Ephesians 4:23).

Another important factor of walking in unconditional love is confessing our faults. We fail too many times because we don't want folks in our business. During my difficult season of mourning a friendship, I learned the importance of accountability. Giving an account of your thoughts and actions to someone else is a humbling but powerful experience. When we confess what we are thinking to someone, it reveals to us the faulty mindsets and attitudes we need to put at the base of the cross. It reminds us of our need for God's forgiveness, which makes it easier to forgive others their trespasses. Scripture is clear when it says:

> Confess your faults one to another, and pray one for another, that ye may be healed. The

effectual fervent prayer of a righteous man availeth much (James 5:16).

The healing that we received is not only physical; it is also the inner healing of our thoughts. The Holy Spirit opens our hearts to see our brothers and sisters correctly. When we need healing on the inside, our view of others will be obscured. We will not see them through the eyes of Christ. Therefore, we will have a critical and unforgiving spirit, which is the breeding ground for bitterness.

> 14 Follow peace with all [men], and holiness, without which no man shall see the Lord:
> 15 Looking diligently lest any man fail of the grace of God; lest any root of bitterness springing up trouble [you], and thereby many be defiled (Hebrews 12:14-15).

We are all filthy rags in the eyes of God but thank God for the sacrifice of Jesus that covers all our wrongs in His blood. I thought I was a forgiving person until I walked the path of unforgiveness. God used a close companion to give me a deeper revelation of His love. We cannot love others as though we have never been hurt if we have not experienced the pain of both hurting and loving simultaneously. It hurts to love unconditionally. Our self-will is the reason for the pain. Our will must bend to the will of God if love is to be matured in us.

Today, I can look back and see how much I have grown in loving others, but I can also see how much more I need to grow in love. As long as we are on this earth, there will always be a deeper level of maturity in the agape love for us to experience. Yes, this means we will have to go through many more seasons of being broken by God. However, we have the benefit of knowing the purpose of the breaking and surrendering to the process. We understand submitting to the breaking, shaping, and pruning without fighting is less painful.

Chapter 18

The Fellowship of Love

And by this shall all men know that ye are my disciples if he ye have love one towards another (John 13:35).

The fellowship of love is probably the most important component of love in my book. Our demonstration of love for each other is what will prove to the world we are indeed disciples of Jesus. Sad to say, what the world sees in the body of Christ currently is a church divided: denominational wars and contentions between members of the same congregation. If we do not present a united front that is born out of love to the world, then the world's view of God will remain obscured.

Fellowship is not about associating with people of your own skin color or doctrinal beliefs. Yet, this is what can be seen in the churches at the moment. The introduction of denominations to distinguish the different schools of thought has done more harm than good. It is unbelievable to hear and see Christians sticking to their own kind racially. In heaven, there will not be a section for the blacks, whites, Hispanics, Asians, Pacific Islanders, and the indigenous people. When God created mankind, He made one species: human beings. It does not matter our color or ancestral backgrounds. We are one people made in the image of God.

True fellowship cannot be achieved if love is not at the core of the relationship. The Greek and Hebrew definitions of fellowship both refer to fellowship as something beyond a surface level relationship. It is much more than our use of the word *koinonia*, which translates into English as the words "communion" or "community." When we have fellowship with God, we can go through life's trials with the joy of the Lord that gives us strength. The fellowship of love is God-directed first before it can be shared with others. We need to come to the place where we are one with God through the fellowship of His suffering as it says in Philippians 3:10:

> 10 I want to know Christ—yes, to know the power of his resurrection and participation in his sufferings, becoming like him in his death

On the night Jesus was betrayed, He washed the disciples' feet and then He gave them a new commandment by saying:

> 34 A new commandment I give unto you, that ye love one another; as I have loved you, that ye also love one another.
>
> 35 By this shall all men know that ye are my disciples, if ye have love one to another (John 13:34-35).

Jesus told His disciples to follow His example by washing each other's feet. The act of foot washing was a sign of servanthood and humility, but it was also about the fellowship of love. Jesus chose to wash the feet of the two men at the table who were going to betray and deny Him on that very night. The Word of God says that love covers a multitude of sins. Washing the feet of His followers was an act of covering the sins of the ones who would betray and deny Him.

Is it possible for us to receive advance notice of denial and betrayal and still love the individuals involved as if we never knew this information? While it is difficult to comprehend, it can be done. It is the very thing Christ is calling us to do. In this same scripture passage, Christ told

His disciples that no servant is greater than His Lord. In other words, if Christ suffered, we, His modern-day followers are going to suffer as well. This is where the fellowship of love is seen.

God is trying to get His children to a place where we will love even if it means pain and death. Many followers of Christ believe Jesus could endure all of the things He did because He is the Son of God. They forget that Jesus was also fully human. Everything He did on the earth was done, not through His deity only but through His humanity that was fully submitted to God.

We tend to forget about the underground churches in China, the Middle East and the countless tragedies that befall Christians in other nations across the globe where persecution is actively taking place. There are men, women, and children standing up for God even if it cost their lives. They have made the decision to suffer for Christ by paying the ultimate price with their lives.

Modern Christianity is watered down, compromised, and self-centered. Christianity is more about being comfortable and finding the right group or clique within the church walls to fit in and become a squad. Jesus had His crew; this is true. But we never see Jesus and His crew as just a social gathering. Whenever we see Jesus and His disciples or even His closet three, He was always about the kingdom and His assignment on the earth. God is looking for people who will step out of modern Christianity and pursue the true essence of Christianity where there is a burden for God and the lost.

It is said that the church is a hospital where saved folks go to get their lives together. While this is true, I believe the best definition I heard of the church is from one of my favorite authors Neil T. Anderson when he said, "The church is a military outpost that has an infirmary." I agree completely. When soldiers enlist in the army, they have a made-up mind that they are going to suffer for the "love" of their country. This is the same type of love God wants us to live out.

Jesus said men will know we are His disciples when we have love one for another. He was not just talking about showing love to each other as Christians, but He was also referring to us, His disciples following in His footsteps. We are to go to the lost and the downtrodden and administer love to them, even when it is not convenient for us. Jesus is implying that love will endure the suffering of being rejected by this world. Yet, we must not take it personally and retaliate. Instead, we must pursue even harder, though it will cause us pain.

The fellowship of love is indeed about community. It is a community of believers who have made up their minds to suffer for the cause of Christ. It is a community of believers who will go beyond the normal and the ordinary to reach the unchurched. We must be a community of believers who have become one with God in suffering by going beyond the modern-day definition of community.

> 12 Beloved, do not be surprised at the fiery trial when it comes upon you to test you, as though some strange thing were happening to you. 13. But rejoice insofar as you share Christ sufferings, that you may also rejoice and be glad when his glory is revealed (1 Peter 4:12-13 ESV).

Sometimes, we forget the Word says trials will come upon us and that we are not to be surprised. The Word also says we must rejoice because we are sharing in the suffering of Christ. If the Word tells us to rejoice, then there must be something about suffering with Christ that is important to us as believers. Could it be that we are missing out because we are constantly complaining when life's trials come? Could it be we are missing the mark because we refuse to submit to the breaking process of God? The breaking process is the best thing God does in our lives.

1 Peter Chapter 4 says the glory of the Spirit of God will come upon us when we suffer, but we must endure the suffering with the right attitude. Peter further tells us that we must not be ashamed to suffer as Christians but we should use our suffering as an opportunity to glorify the name of God. It is hard to find something to glorify God about when we are under extreme pressure, but if we think about the price paid on Calvary, we will always find something to be grateful for.

We will never be able to glorify God from a place of joy if we don't allow the fellowship of love to flow out of our lives. The fellowship of love is contingent upon our walk with Christ on a daily basis. If the flesh is dominating our lives day in and day out then it will be hard to have fellowship with God, let alone our brothers and sisters in Christ.

The fellowship of love allows us to grow closer to God, which in turn opens up the river of love to flow to others. When love is in operation, we will not consider our sufferings for Christ as a difficult thing to walk through. Love is needed for every area of our Christian walk. Love is the key to knowing God more intimately than we first knew Him at our salvation new birth experience.

Conclusion

The Greatest Commandment

> 35 Then one of them, which was a lawyer, asked him a question, tempting him, and saying, 36 Master, which is the great commandment in the law? 37 Jesus said unto him, Thou, shalt love the Lord thy God with all thy heart, and with all thy soul, and with all thy mind. 38 This is the first and great commandment. 39 And the second is like unto it, Thou, shalt love thy neighbour as thyself. 40 On these two commandments hang all the law and the prophets (Matthew 22:35-40).

The Pharisees and the Sadducees were always trying to get Jesus to mess up and say something wrong. However, Jesus was always ahead of them and knew exactly what it was they were trying to accomplish. In this encounter, the Pharisees who felt they were superior asked Jesus what He thought the greatest commandment was. Jesus responded with the above-mentioned scripture.

As disciples of Jesus, we are to live out the very words Christ spoke to the Pharisees and the crowd that were gathered around. We are to love the Lord our God with all of our hearts, souls, and minds. Jesus said this is the greatest commandment. He further stated that loving our neighbors as ourselves is the second greatest commandment. If Jesus said that we are to love our neighbors as ourselves then why aren't we doing it? There are two reasons:

1. We have not gotten to the place where we love God with our entire being
2. We do not love ourselves

Love cannot and will not flow from vessels that have blockages. We must walk in the freedom Christ purchased for us on Calvary so that we can walk in this commandment to love with our entire beings. When we learn how to love from our hearts, souls, and minds, then we can share that love with others.

The Bible says the heart of man is desperately wicked. There is no good thing in us. Even when we think we are being good, God says our righteousness is as filthy rags.

Our souls are very worldly; therefore, they are always seeking carnal things. The pleasures of this world are only temporal; yet, our souls insist on partaking in these things because the soul loves instant gratification. This is the reason why scripture teaches us the soul that sins shall surely die. The soul that is not surrendered to Jesus is slowly being poisoned and eventually, it will die. Anything that is not connected to the living, life-giving Jesus will die and be eternally separated from God the Father.

Our minds are playgrounds for the Devil. He takes great pleasure in keeping us trapped in our minds with self-defeating thoughts. If we don't learn the schemes and the tricks of the Enemy, a stronghold will eventually develop and take root in our minds. When a stronghold has taken hold, it is very hard for us to remove it. I believe strongholds are hard to be seen in our lives because they become so entangled and concealed. When we search our minds for the source of our negative thinking it's often hard to find. If by happenstance we do recognize our place of bondage, the entanglement is so strong it's near impossible to break free.

All of us must give Christ full access to our lives by allowing Him to sit on the throne of our hearts. Our hearts are the central command headquarters of our lives. The issues of life flow from our hearts. When Christ reigns as the king on the throne of our hearts, He sets out to reclaim the territories occupied by the Enemy. These territories are the soul and mind.

> For to set the mind on the flesh is death, but to set the mind on the spirit is life and peace (Romans 8:6).

Clearly, we can see that when our minds are on the worldly things or the things of the flesh, it will eventually lead to death. This death is both physical and spiritual. However, those who set their minds on the things of God will have life and peace.

> Finally, brethren, whatsoever things are true, whatsoever things are honest, whatsoever things are just, whatsoever things are pure, whatsoever things are lovely, whatsoever things are of good report; if there be any virtue, and if there be any praise, think on these things (Philippians 4:8).

The key to keeping a healthy mind is focusing it on Christ. When we concentrate on the things of Christ, our minds have no room to pay attention to the carnal things.

It is important that as Christians we understand this. Our hearts, souls, and minds are to be fully surrendered and submitted to Christ. Many Christians are surrendered to Christ, but they have not submitted. When we are not submitted to God, we constantly fight what He is doing in our lives. Questioning His authority in our lives shows we are not submitted. The excuses we come up with to remain the same is evidence of our failure to submit.

Finally, we do not show genuine love for others because we are fighting internal battles to accept ourselves. When we disregard our values to fit into societal constructs, it shows a lack of love and appreciation for self. How can we love our neighbors as ourselves if we are constantly seeking the approval of others?

We have placed too much power into the hands of other people, and we compromise our opinions to fit in with the culture. This culture is not always right. In fact, the things that are being portrayed in this current world culture do not depict the values of God. Yet, many Christians are following hard after the world's standards. Many are walking around with unforgiveness, not for others but self. We are so hard on ourselves at times and refuse to let go of the mistakes we tend to make as humans. Unforgiveness towards self stems from a lack of self-love. Love is the catalyst that causes forgiveness to operate.

If you are having a hard time forgiving someone, it's because you are not walking in love. Love will always be quick to forgive and cover faults. Love keeps no record of wrongs. If you live in your past failures and are constantly feeling guilty over the said shortcomings, it means your love walk is damaged. We cannot love God with our entire beings when our love walk is damaged.

Our seasons of brokenness mature the seed of love that is inside every believer called agape love. It is not easy for love to spout and grow rapidly, for there are weeds and thorns present in our hearts that must be gutted out and trashed. Love needs a lot of room to grow and spread. There is a vine called the love vine, which will grow and take over anything. The love vine never dies by itself. It will continue to spread and gain ground if it is not controlled.

The love of God unlike the love vine in the natural cannot and will not die. The love of God will grow, mature, and flourish in our lives because God will take us through numerous cycles of breaking, pruning, and crushing until love is fully matured. As stated throughout this book, the breaking, pruning, and crushing process can be as long or as short as possible. The duration of our brokenness depends on our co-operation with God. The more stubborn and strong-willed we are, the more pain we will experience.

I think I have had my fill of being stubborn to the will of God for my life. It took me too many years and too many cycles to realize that God is not trying to kill me (rolling my eyes). With every season of pain I have gone through, He is refining and maturing me into His character of love. The many tears I have shed throughout the years are a witness to love's transformation journey in me.

I congratulate you for getting to the end of the book. God is truly amazing, and His Word, the Bible, is indeed a treasure map. I have heard so many teachings about God crushing and breaking us to produce the anointing, but the secret of it all is love.

1 Corinthians Chapter 13 is the greatest secret in plain sight, for we often read it but still miss its message. This chapter is about the Christian character, which is the character of God. Whatever we do for God must be done in love. God is saying that if we still think this life is about us then we are children. Children, in their innocence, lack understanding in some areas and cannot see past their present needs. Mature people know what it is to set aside their

feelings for the common good. When we mature in love, our whole outlook on life changes. We see people differently. We will truly see all men as Christ sees them. The Christian journey is about faith, hope, and love but the greatest of the three is love.

God is committed to us. Hence, He will never remove the love He has for us. We must see ourselves differently to begin to love ourselves. There are many wonderful things God has said about us in His Word that we need to start believing and applying to our broken places. Love God with your entire being and then let that love transform your thinking so that it will flow to others. This new commandment requires removing the veil from our eyes to see our value in God and by extension, God's love for mankind.

Spiritual Inventory

There comes a time when we must take spiritual inventory of our lives. This spiritual inventory can be performed at any time on the Christian journey. It will help keep us on track, and to recognize when we are in the seasons of breaking, pruning, and crushing.

The following questions can be used at any time to determine whether or not we are about to enter a breaking season or in a breaking season. There are many more signs that can help us to evaluate our spiritual condition but these are just a few to get you started. There are spaces provided so you can answer each question. I suggest you use a journal to answer the questions as they can open up the flood gates so to speak.

1. Are you feeling inadequate in your spiritual life?

2. Are you hiding from others what's really going on inside?

3. Can you blend into a crowd but still feel alone on this earth?

4. Do your conversations with God feel strained at the moment?

5. Are you taking on too many projects just so you won't have time to deal with what's happening on the inside?

6. Are you overly sensitive?

7. Is rejection still seen as an enemy instead of a blessing?

8. Are there walls with posted signs saying "Keep Out" surrounding your heart?

9. Do you read the Bible but the words don't connect or stick in your mind?

10. Is your heart fully submitted to God or are you still fighting to remain in control?

Prayer of confession and submission to the will of God

God, I come to You thanking You for all You have done in my life up to this point. Everything seems to be going crazy and turned upside down in my life at the moment. I must confess that I have often blamed You for life's situations that have left me broken. I have walked away from You too many times because I want to control my life.

Father, forgive me for not submitting to the process You have begun in my life. Forgive me for complaining and giving up too easily. I ask for Your forgiveness because of my blindness and a nasty attitude. I didn't learn the lessons You tried to teach me, so I went around in circles.

Father, remove the scales from my eyes so I can see clearly as I surrender my heart, soul, mind, body to You. Father, I choose to deny myself, take up my cross and follow You daily. I understand now that You are trying to refine my character so that I look like You in my actions and speech.

Father, as I commune with You from this day forward, may my eyes always be on You, not life's circumstances. God, may the testimony that is my life be a witness to others who are currently broken by the sin nature and can't see a way of escape. May my life be a living witness to the saints who are currently going through being broken by You. Father, let them know it's only for a time and a season.

Father, may the seed of love that is within each believer reading this book begin to grow and mature as You refine our lives to look more like You. May each sinner who picks up this book understand the love You have for this broken world and turn to You as Savior. May we as a body seek to walk in unconditional love just as Your Son Jesus. For it is by our love this world will see You and us as Your true disciples. Father, I pray all these things in the name of Your Son Jesus the Christ my risen Savior and soon coming King. Amen.

Other Publications by this Author

Have you ever taken an honest look at yourself and the different experiences life allowed you walk through and questioned the reason for them all? Have you had that soul-searching look within yourself only to discover there are secrets hidden beneath the surface? In *Caged: Your Scars His Purpose,* the author takes a journey of self-introspection and discovers something unbelievable that will lead her to the One person who can work everything out for good. Life's experiences shape us into the people we are today, and teach us many lessons. We must share these valuable lessons with others walking the same paths we once navigated. Orencia's shares her own life story of self-discovery to empower you to be able to share your story with others and bring healing and deliverance from secret pains you carry.

Find out what happens when Jaime and Sam decide to play Lifeguards in this hilarious story about having an overactive imagination.

Connection Time

Connect with and follow Orencia R. Bulze on social media platforms

www.facebook.com/yourscarshispurpose

www.instagram.m/orbulze

www.twitter.com/orbulze

www.goodreads.com/orbulze

Orencia would love to hear from you, especially your thoughts on this subject matter.

You can reach her at the above-mentioned social media platforms or through her website or email address.

www.orbulze.com

Scars.purpose@gmail.com

Orbulze@gmail.com

I would appreciate it very much if you leave me a review on Amazon.

About the Author

Orencia Bulze is a native of the island of St. Vincent and the Grenadines. She is an author and a speaker on a mission to help people see the reality of their dreams. Through her first work, *Caged: Your Scars, His Purpose*, she became known for her candor in recounting the experiences of her life.

Rency, as she is affectionately called, is a woman of faith with a penchant for children's literature that ultimately caused her to publish an illustrated children's book, *Lifeguard J.E.T.*

Connect with Orencia on Facebook or Instagram to learn about new releases and future events.

www.ingramcontent.com/pod-product-compliance
Lightning Source LLC
LaVergne TN
LVHW090116080426
835507LV00040B/906